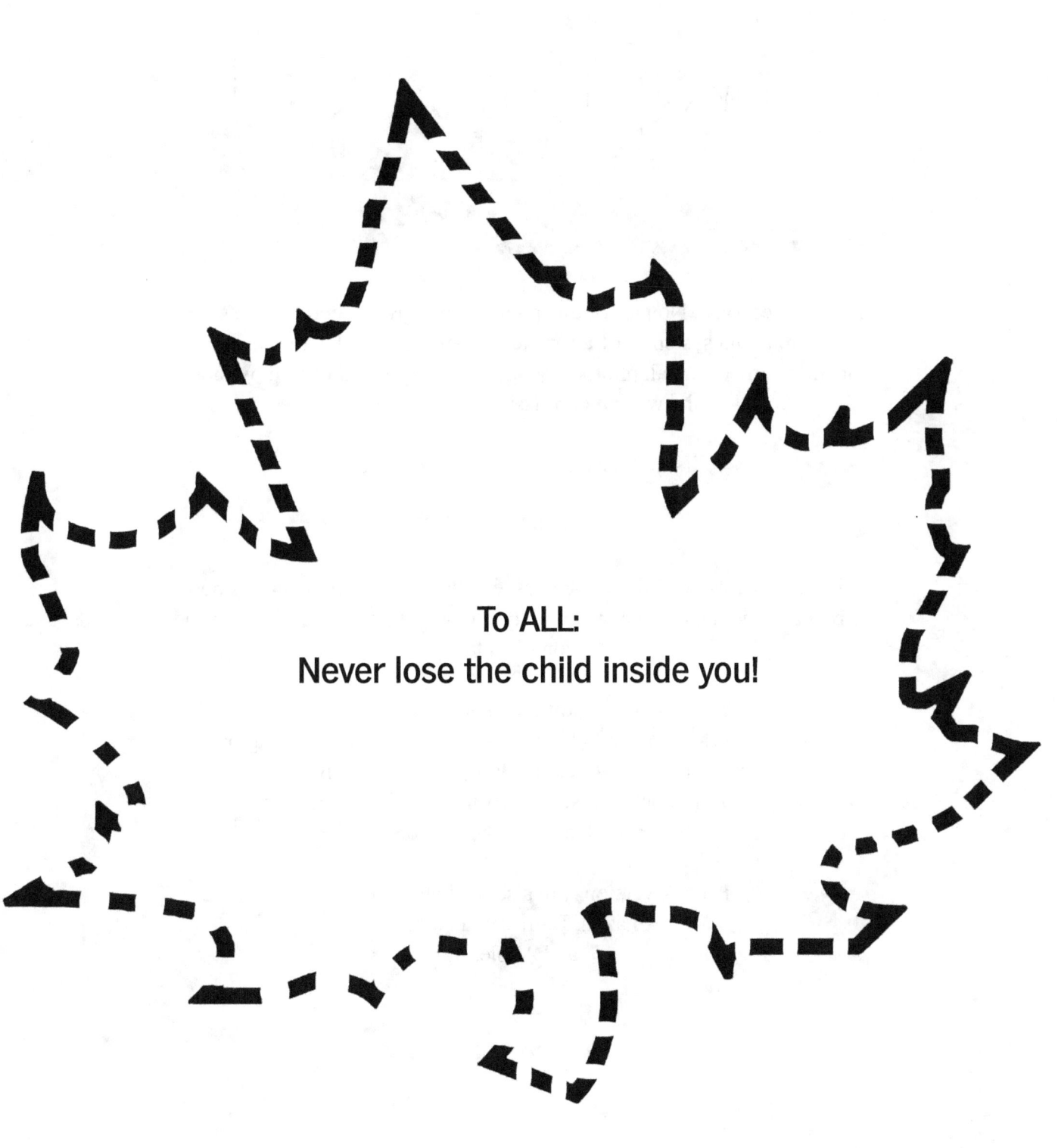

To ALL:

Never lose the child inside you!

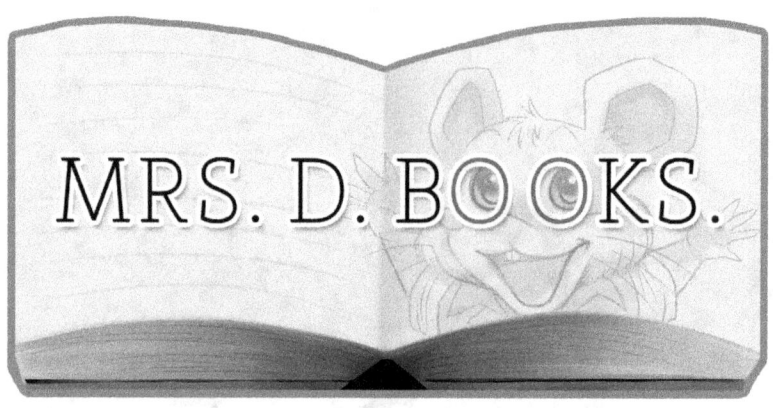
First published by Mrs. D. Books LLC

ISBN: 978-1984956323

To order additional paperback or
hardcover copies of "That Is How Things Are," or this coloring book,
please visit Amazon.com, Barnesandnoble.com, or
the author's website, www.mrsdbooks.net or
email olga@mrsdbooks.com

E-book versions are also available through
Amazon, Barnes and Noble,
and Apple.

That Is How Things Are

PREFACE

Settle down in warm surroundings and get your crayons and pencils ready, because this coloring book will revise your inner list! It's based on the book "That Is How Things Are," which explains the cycle of life to children. It movingly captures the soul of fall through the powerful wind, departing leaves, chilly air, and busy squirrels looking for the last acorns. The dramatic instructive artwork will introduce young readers and artists to the powerful wind and how autumn changes to winter. The beautiful illustrations will move young children into a state of wonder, which is hard to resist. The unique characters from the two stories will make children think about the power of nature and life outside.

If possible, please read the story first. I hope that by the end of the reading or coloring journey, the young explorers will rush outside to discover nature, just as the little kitten did. As they take a closer look at the most dramatic force, the wind, they will learn about changes from one season to another. This powerful narrative will take them to the sky, from where children can observe the drastic changes transforming the beautiful golden autumn to winter. The sights and feelings many children experience during the transition from fall to winter inspire youngsters to observe the world around them. This is an ideal story (and artwork) for home, classroom, and bedtime reading all year long.

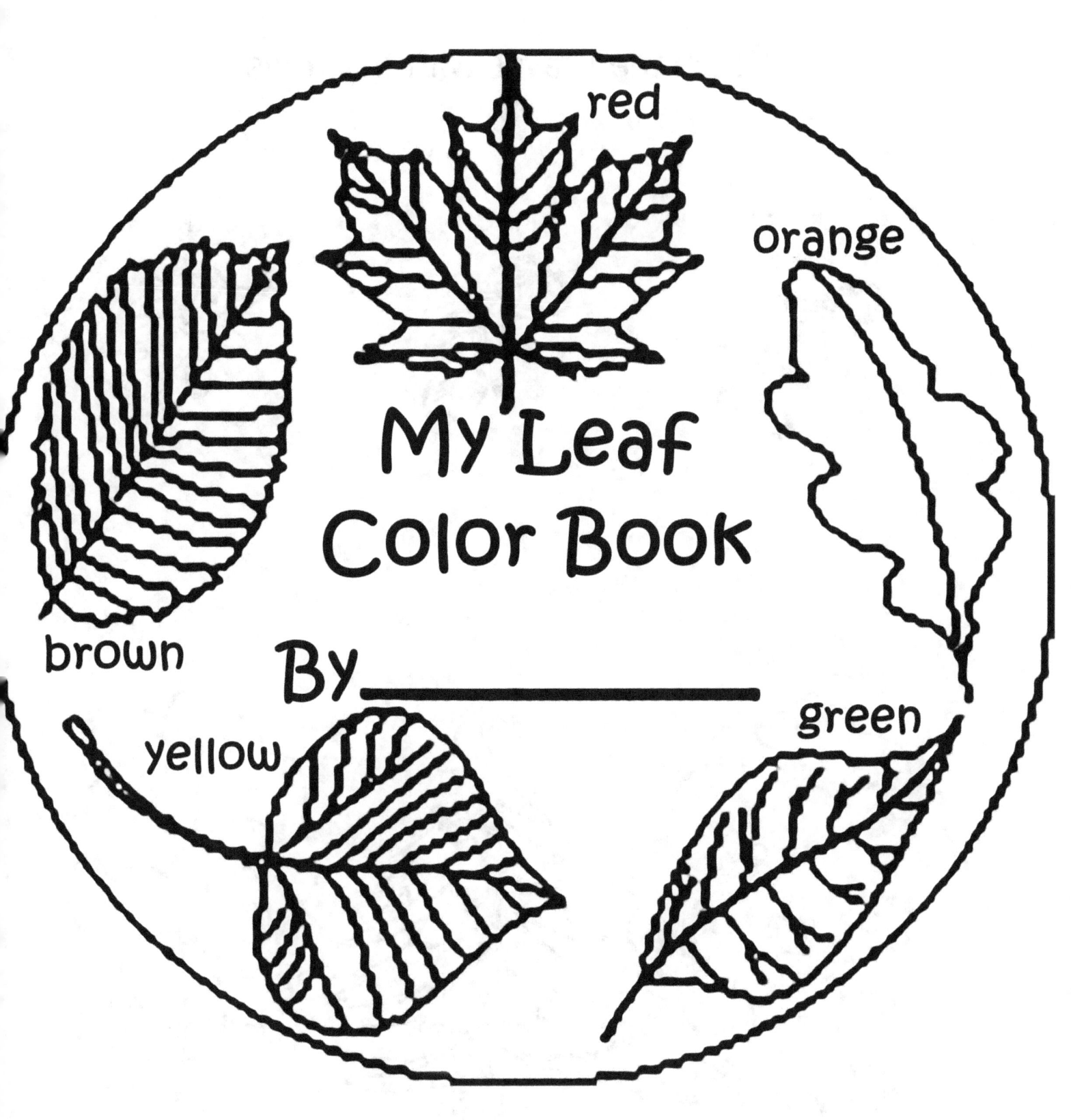

red

orange

My Leaf
Color Book

brown

By _____

green

yellow

Match the Leaves with the Trees

PINE TREE   BIRCH   OAK

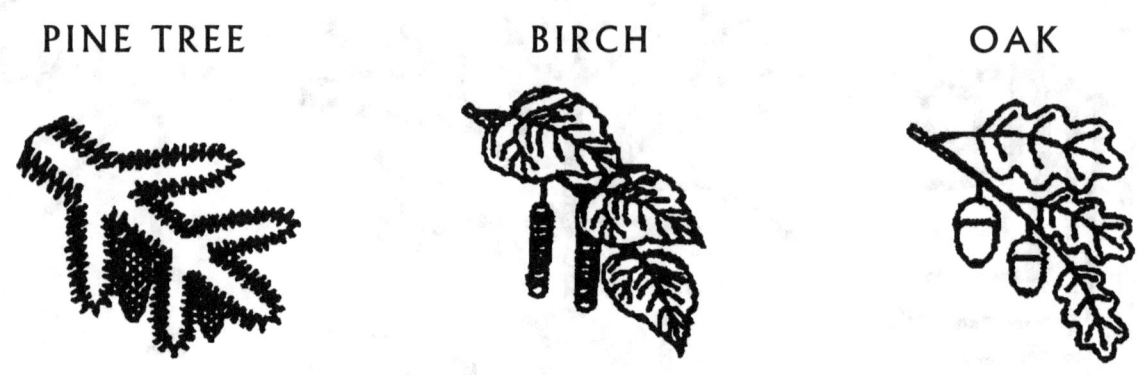

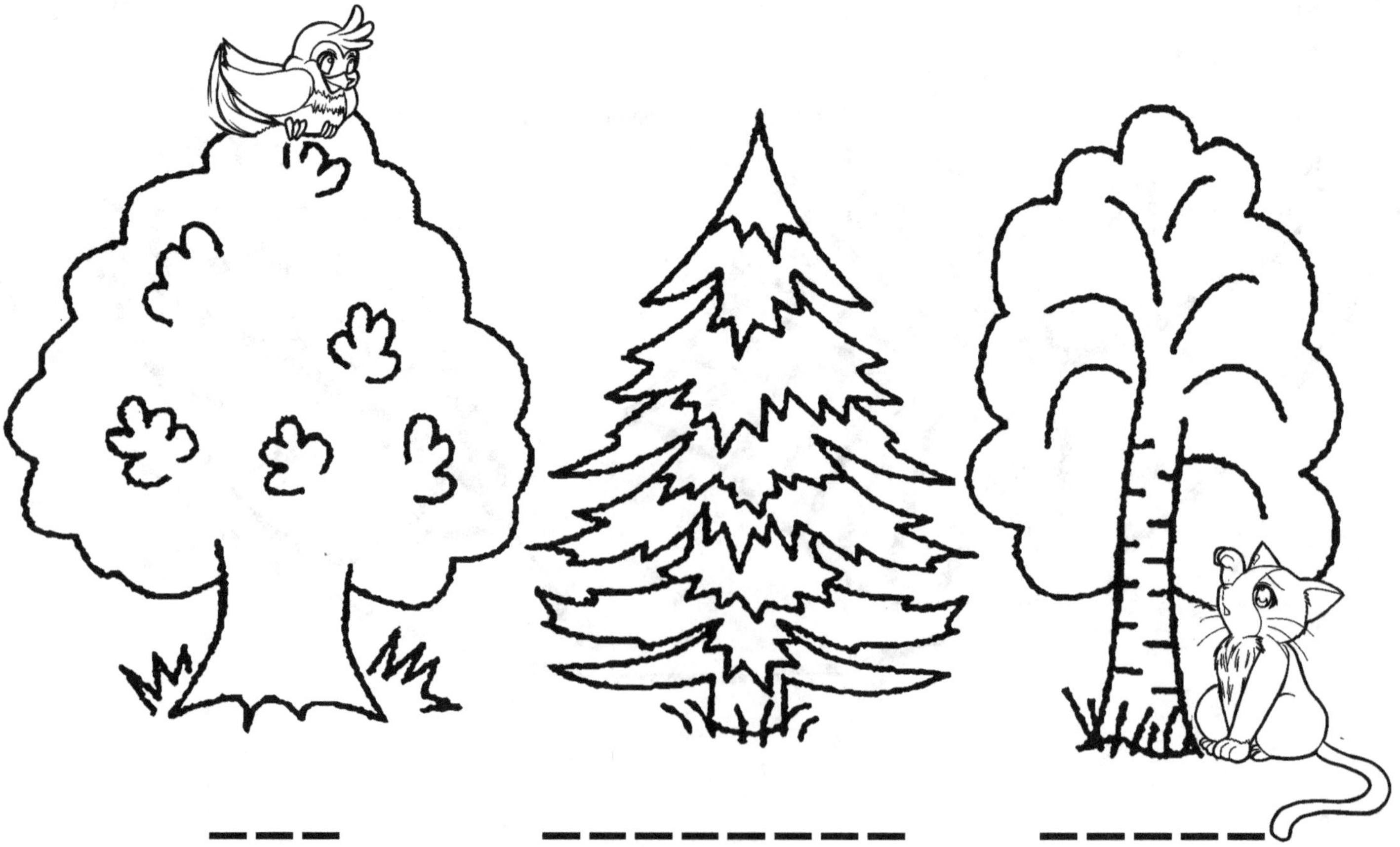

_ _ _   _ _ _ _ _ _ _ _   _ _ _ _ _ _

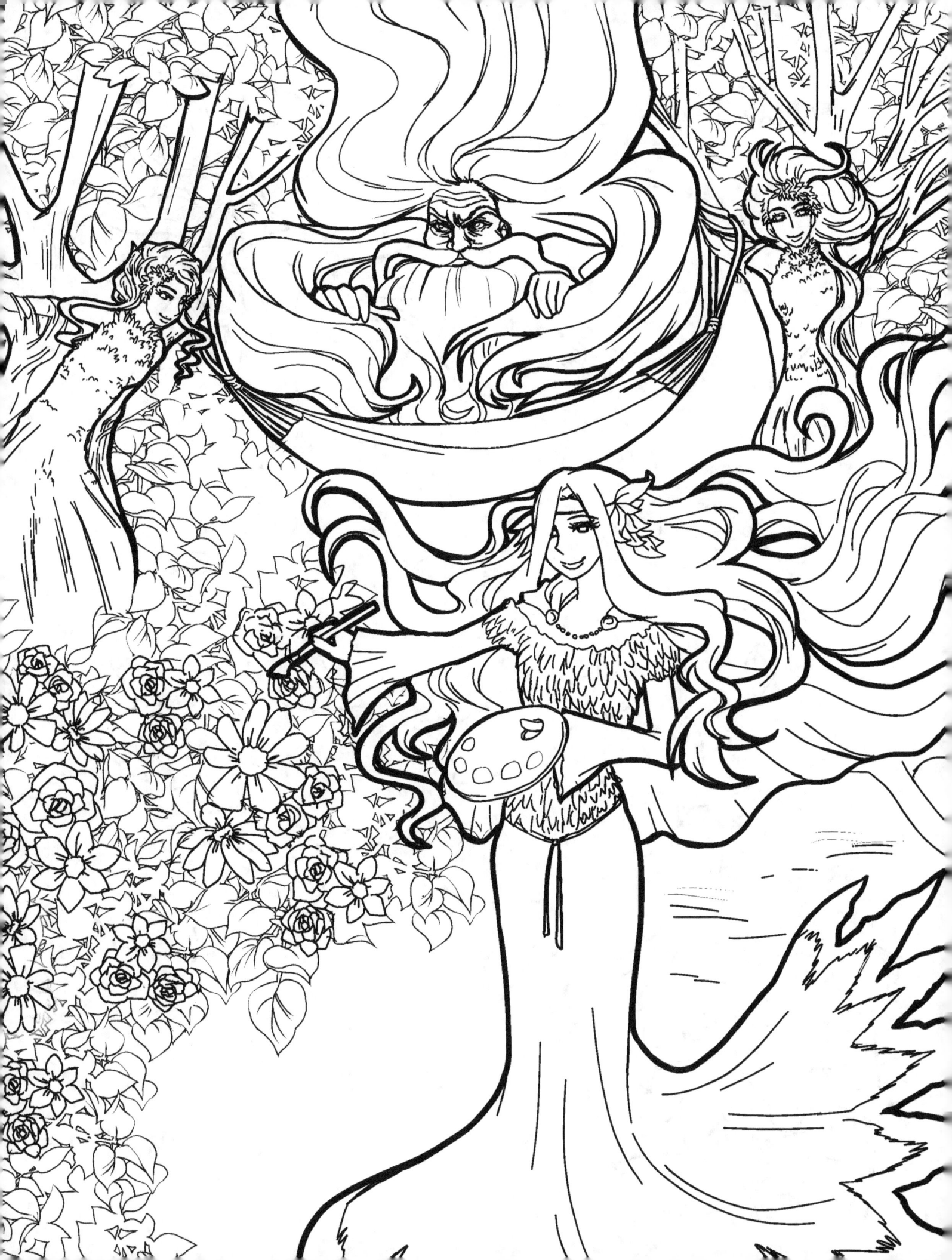

Follow the Leaves

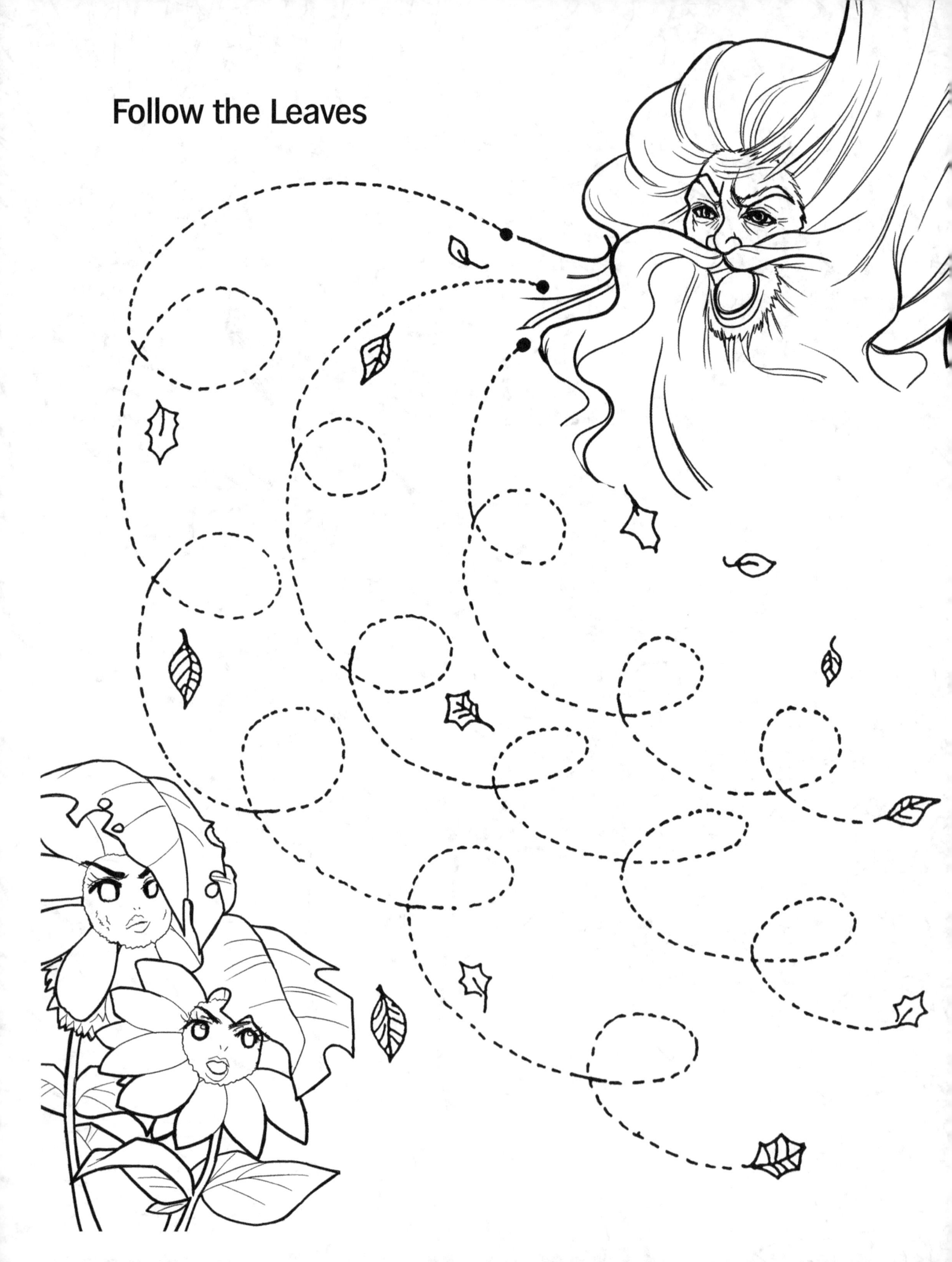

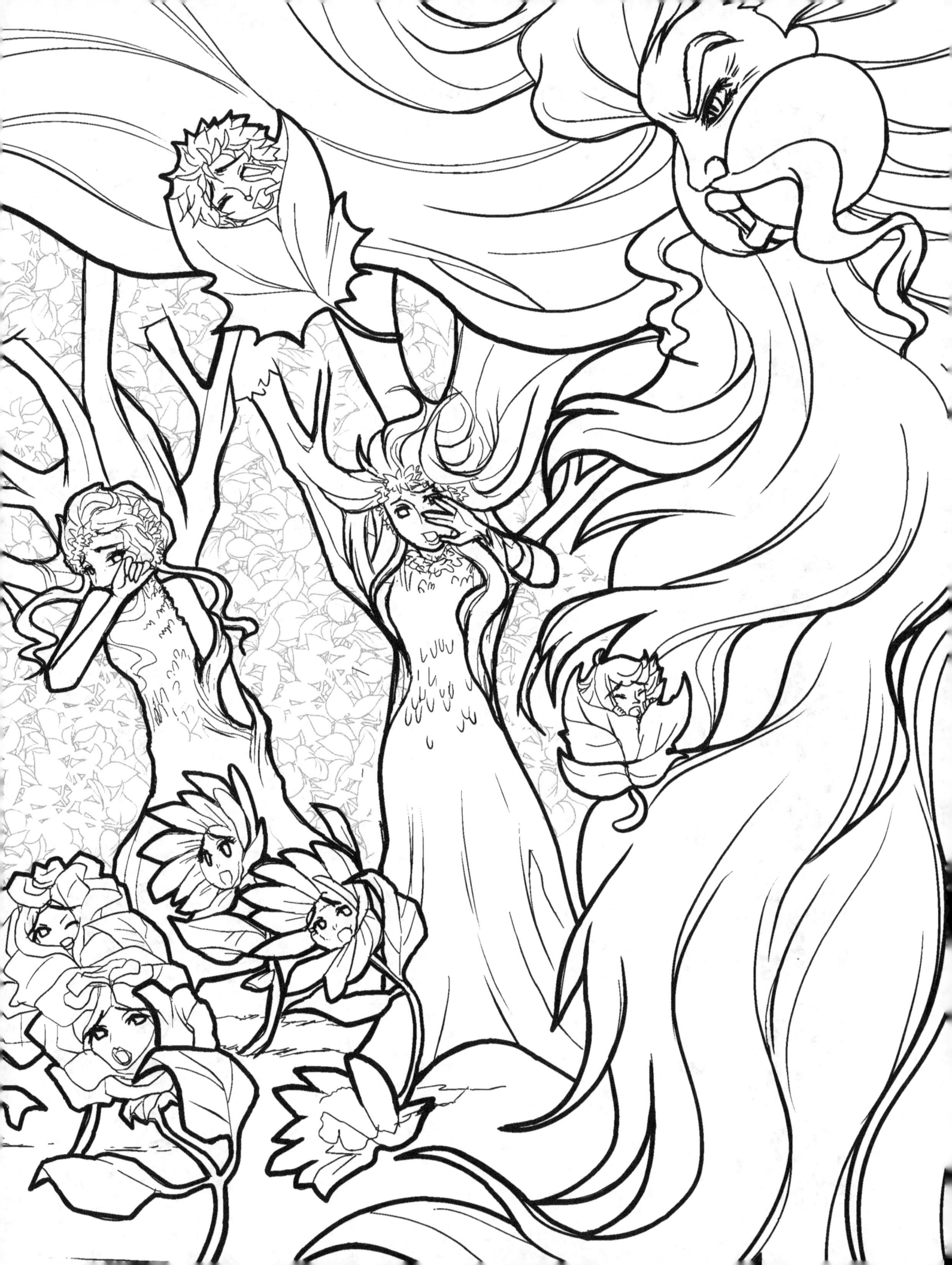

Connect All Matching Leaves

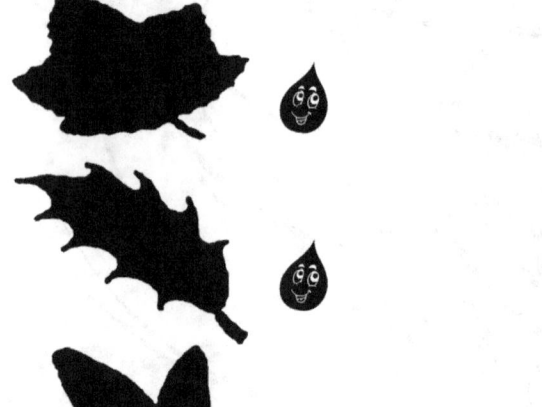
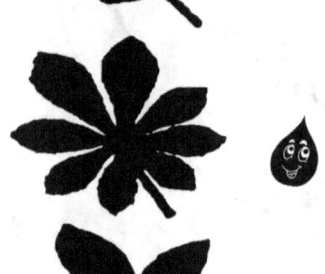

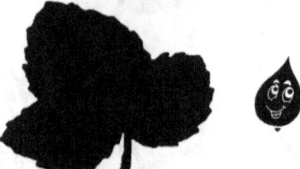
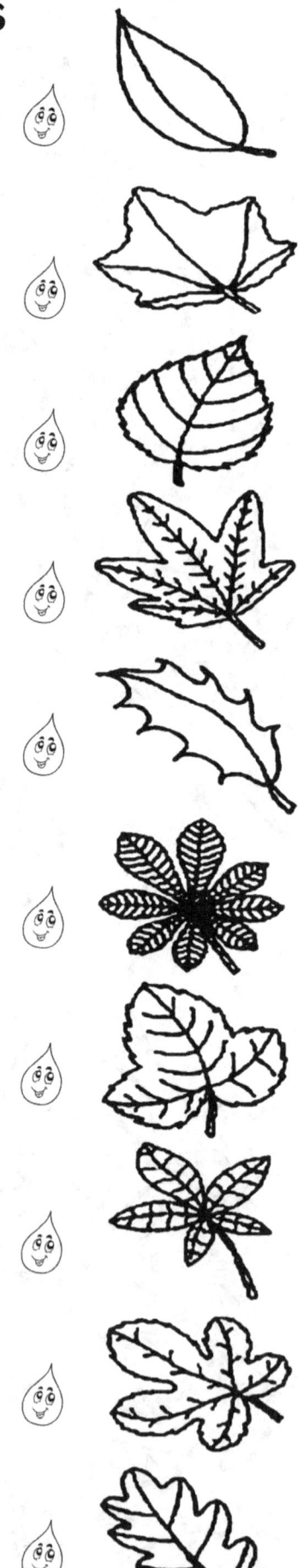

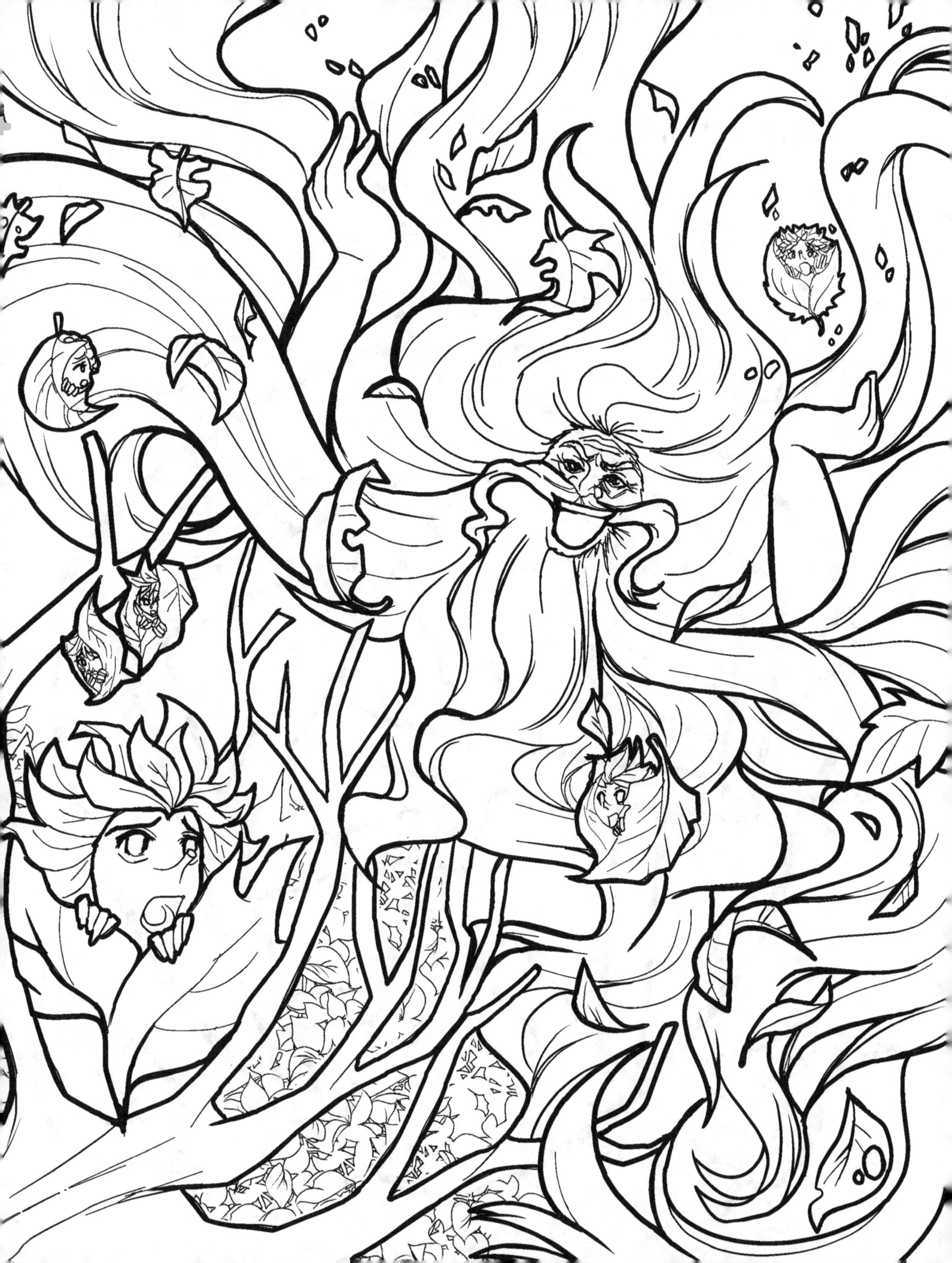

Start and Finish!

Start

Finish!

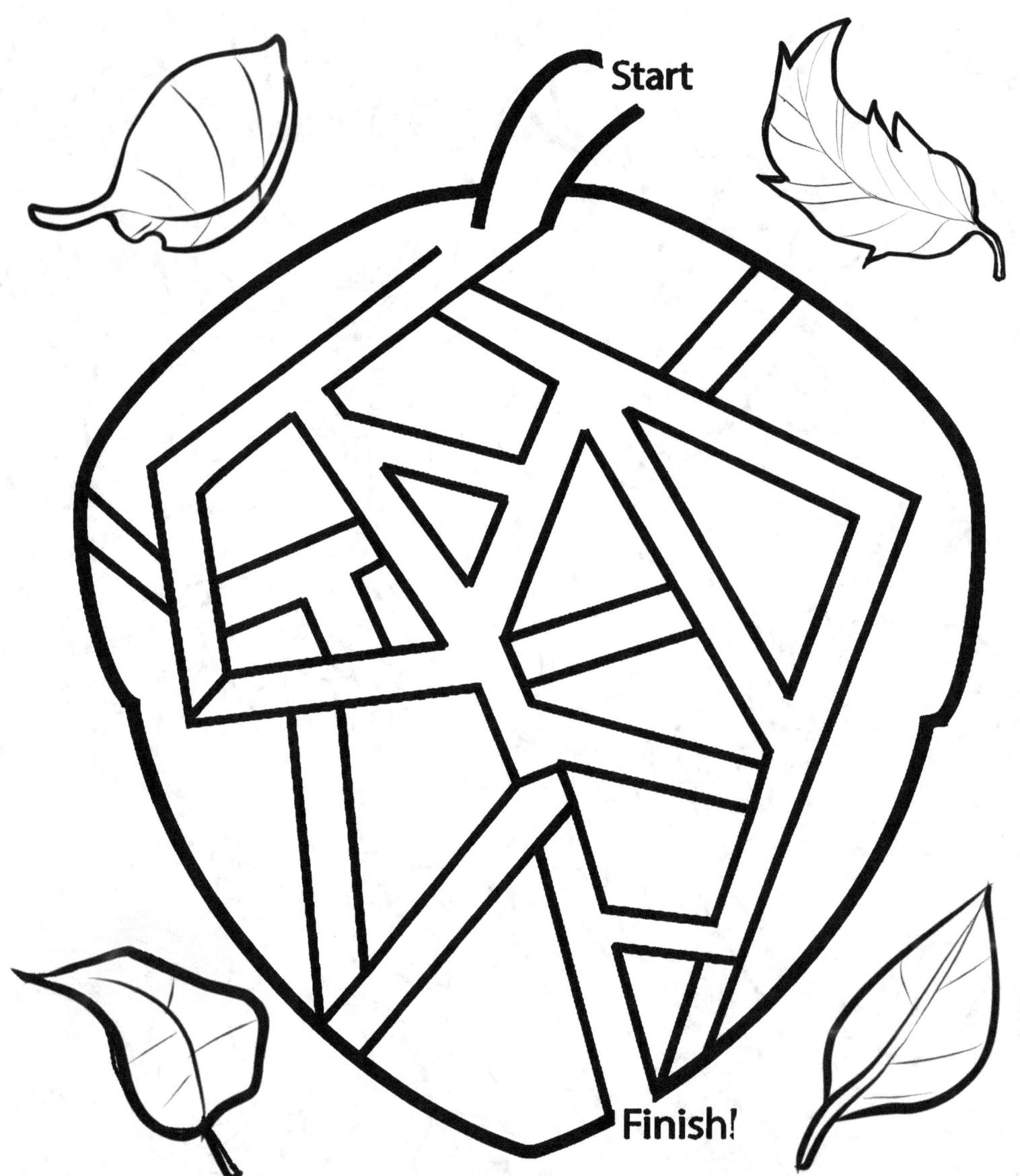

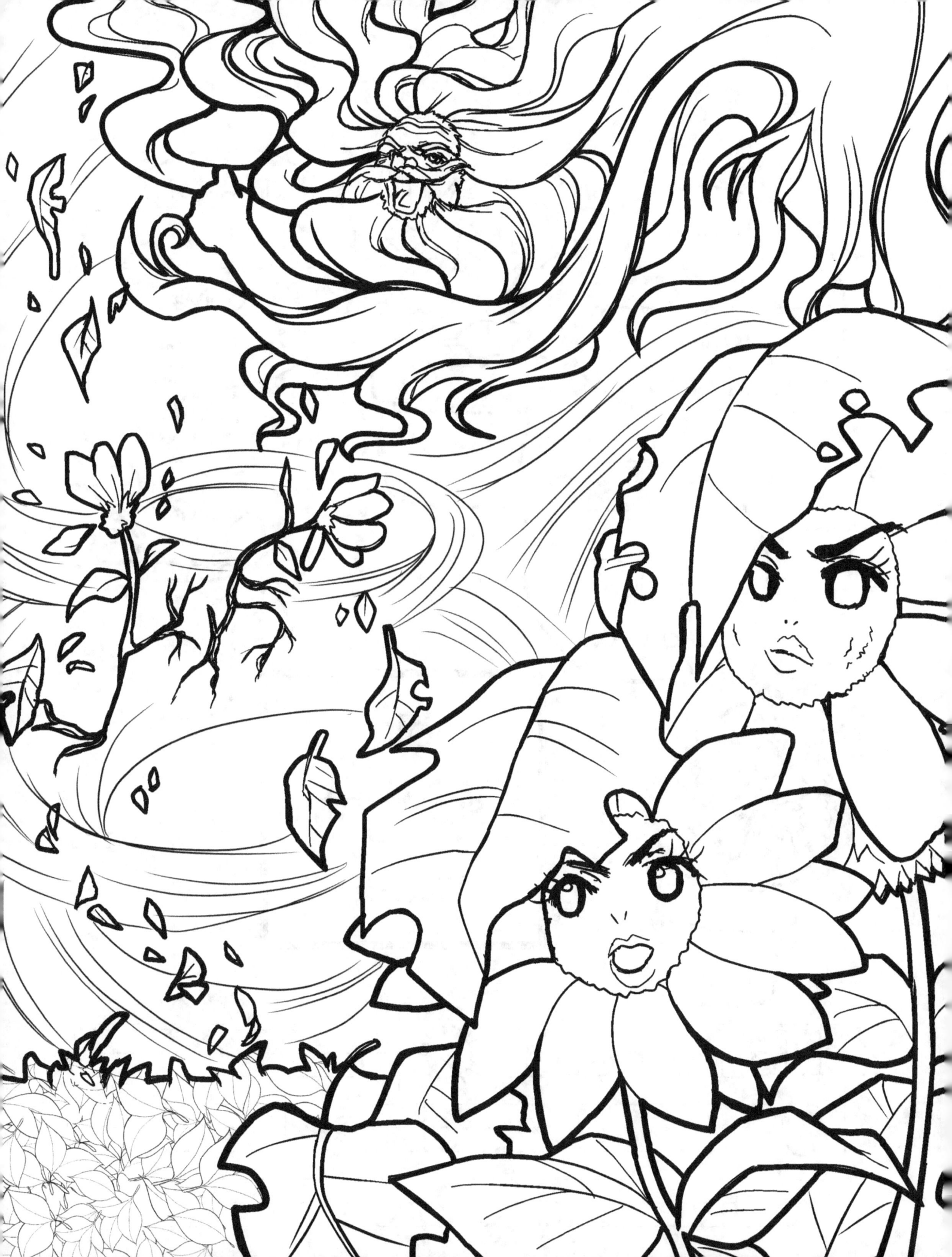

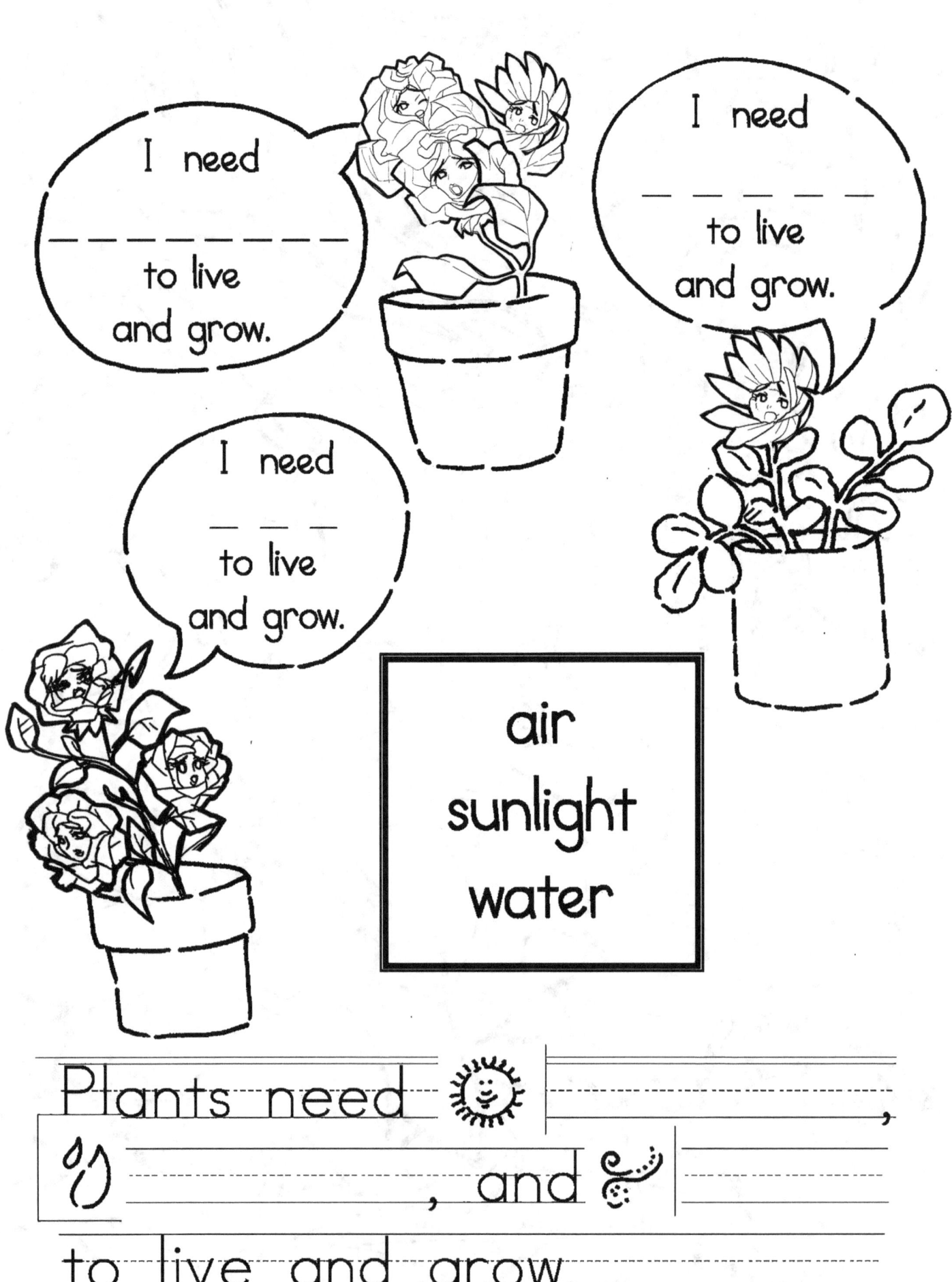

I need
_ _ _ _ _
to live
and grow.

I need
_ _ _ _ _
to live
and grow.

I need
_ _ _
to live
and grow.

air
sunlight
water

Plants need ☀ _____,
💧 _____, and 🌀 _____
to live and grow.

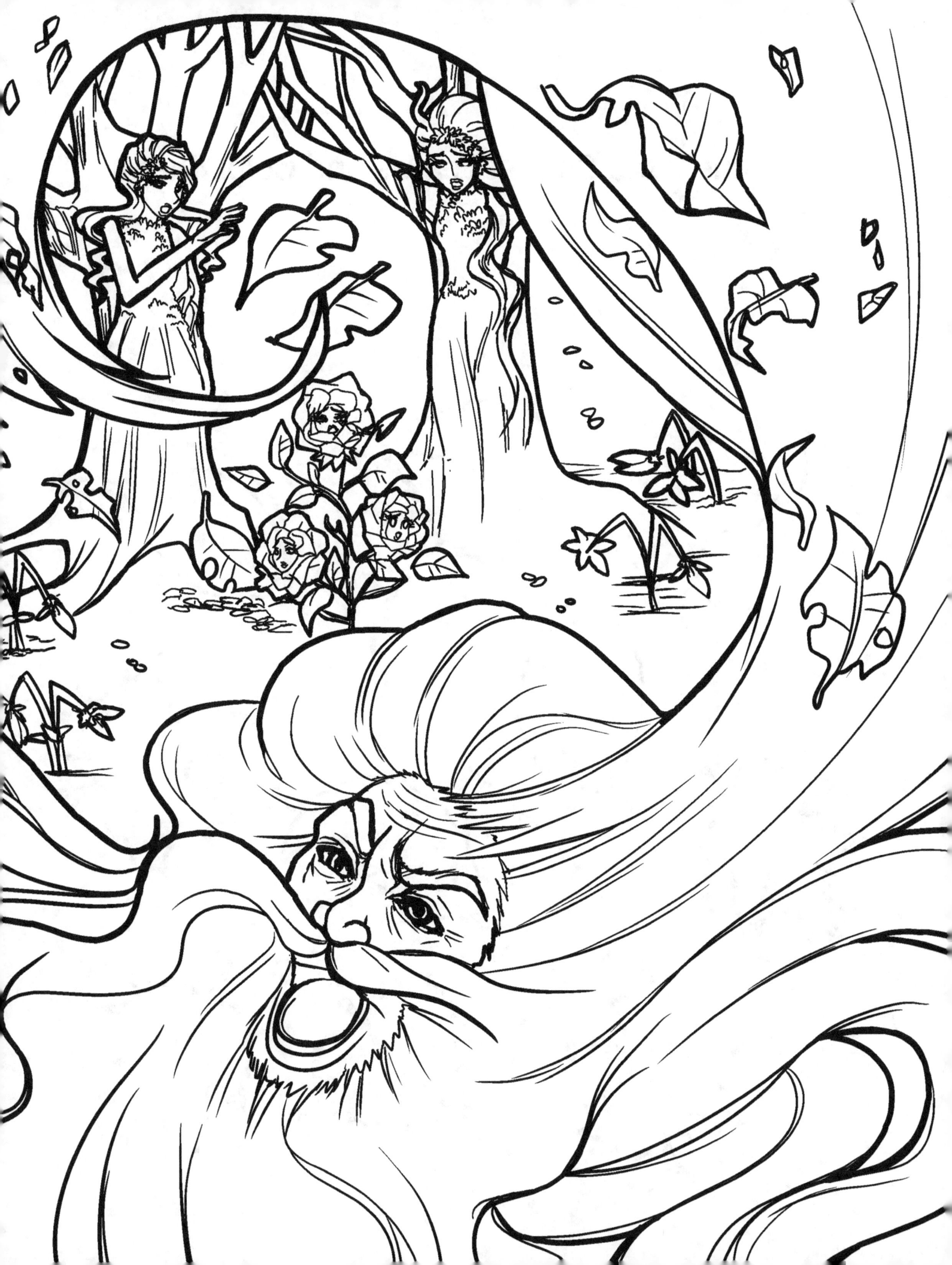

Connect the Correct Leaves and Color Them!

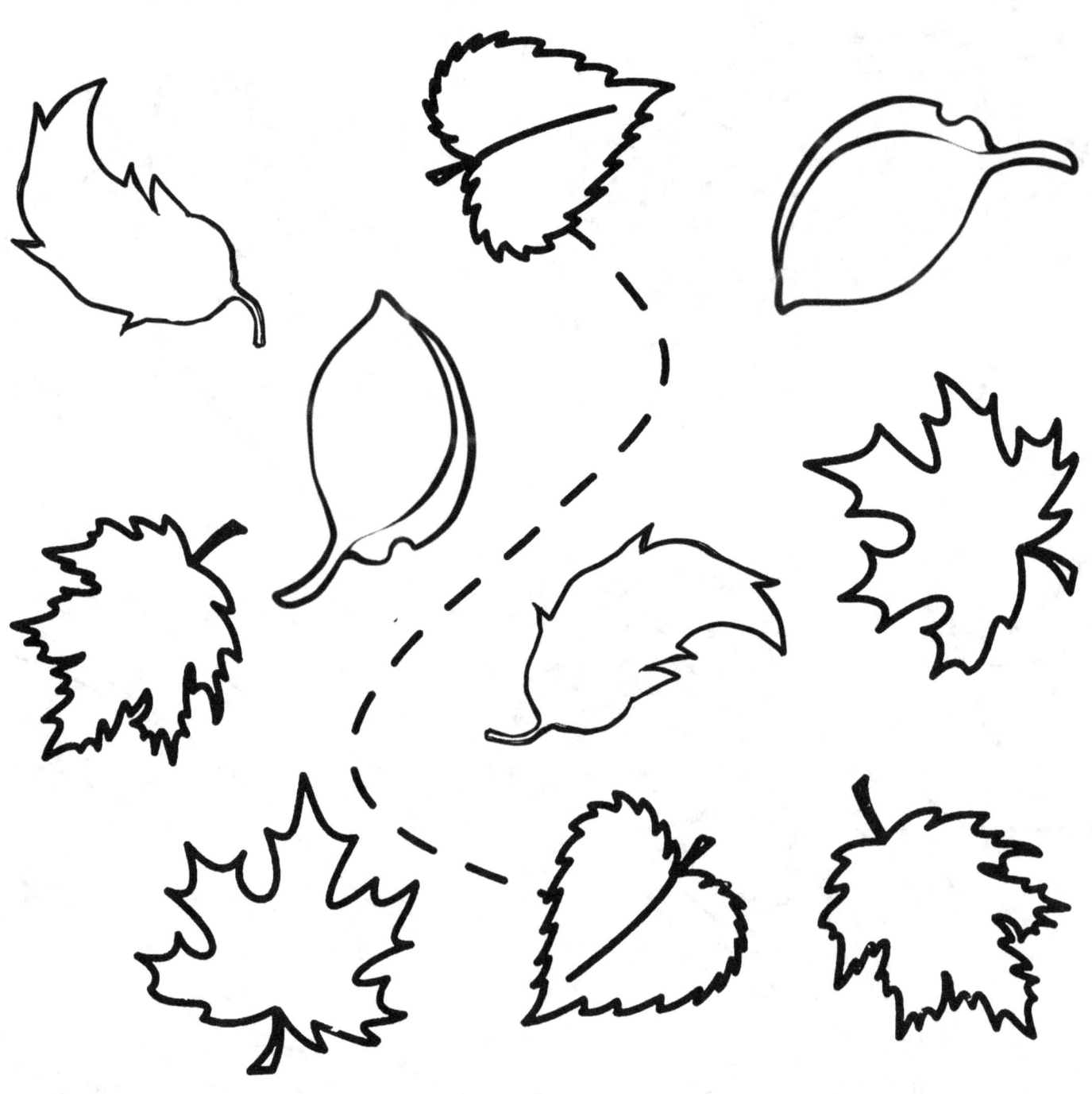

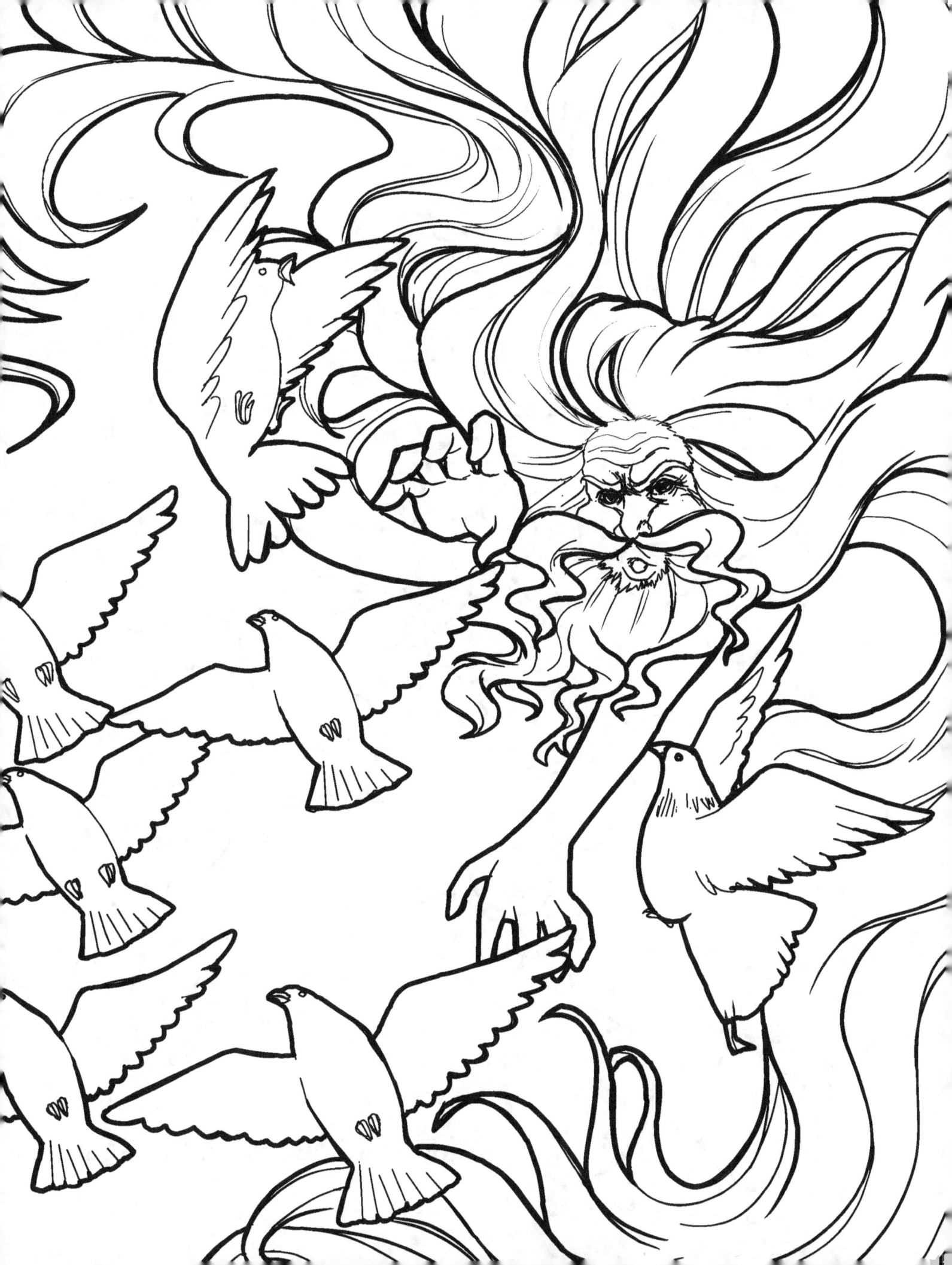

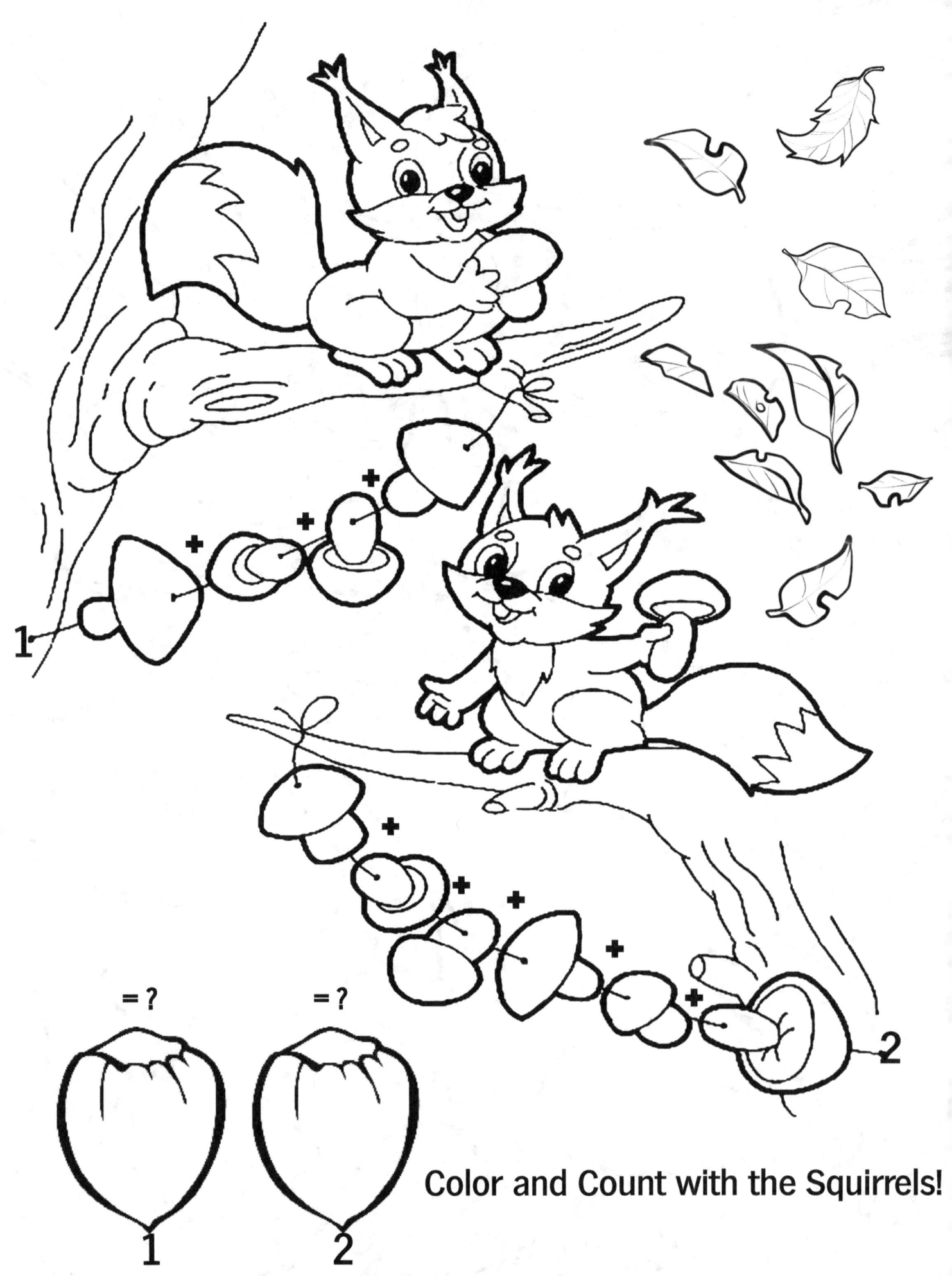

Color and Count with the Squirrels!

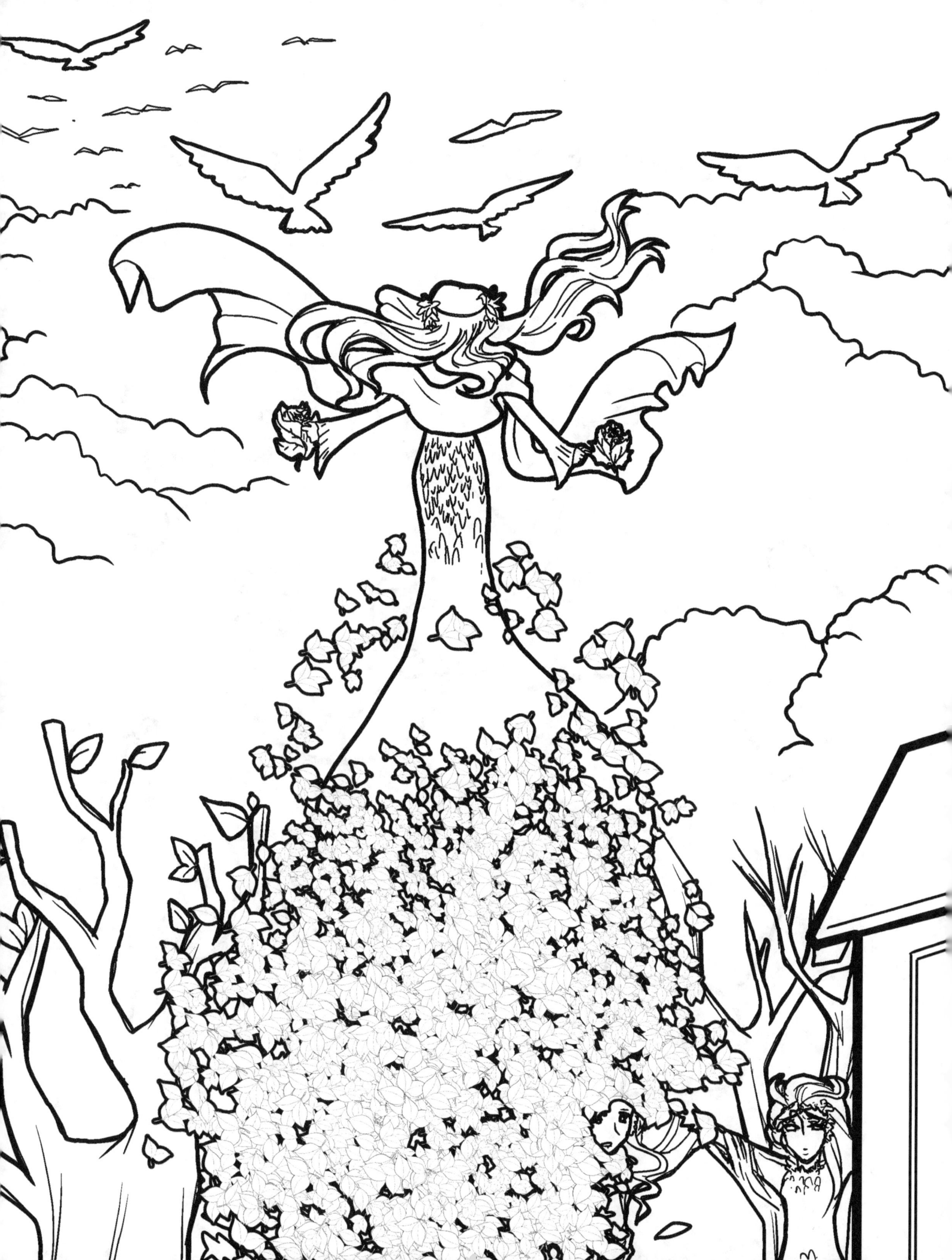

Connect All Dots and Color!

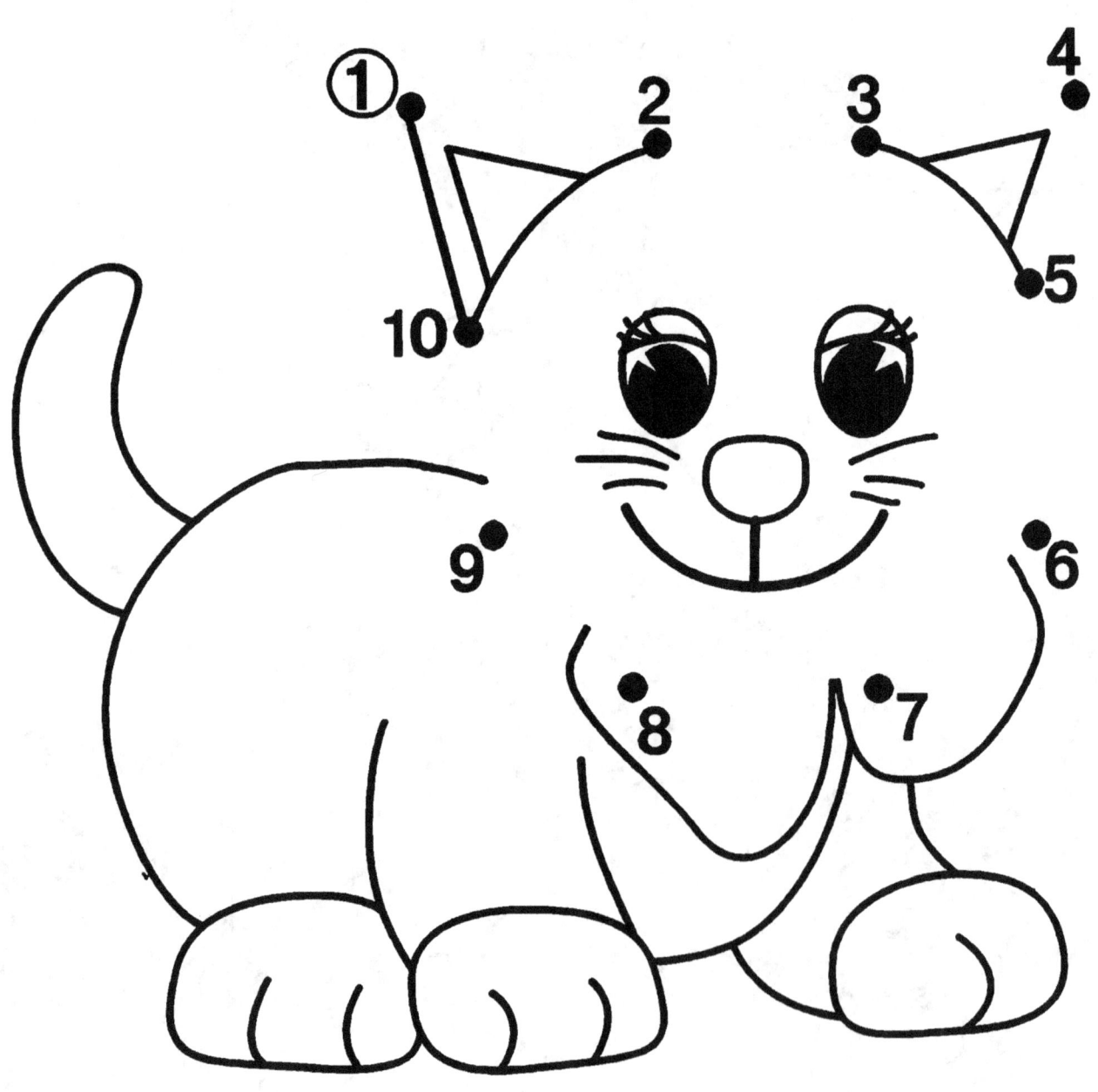

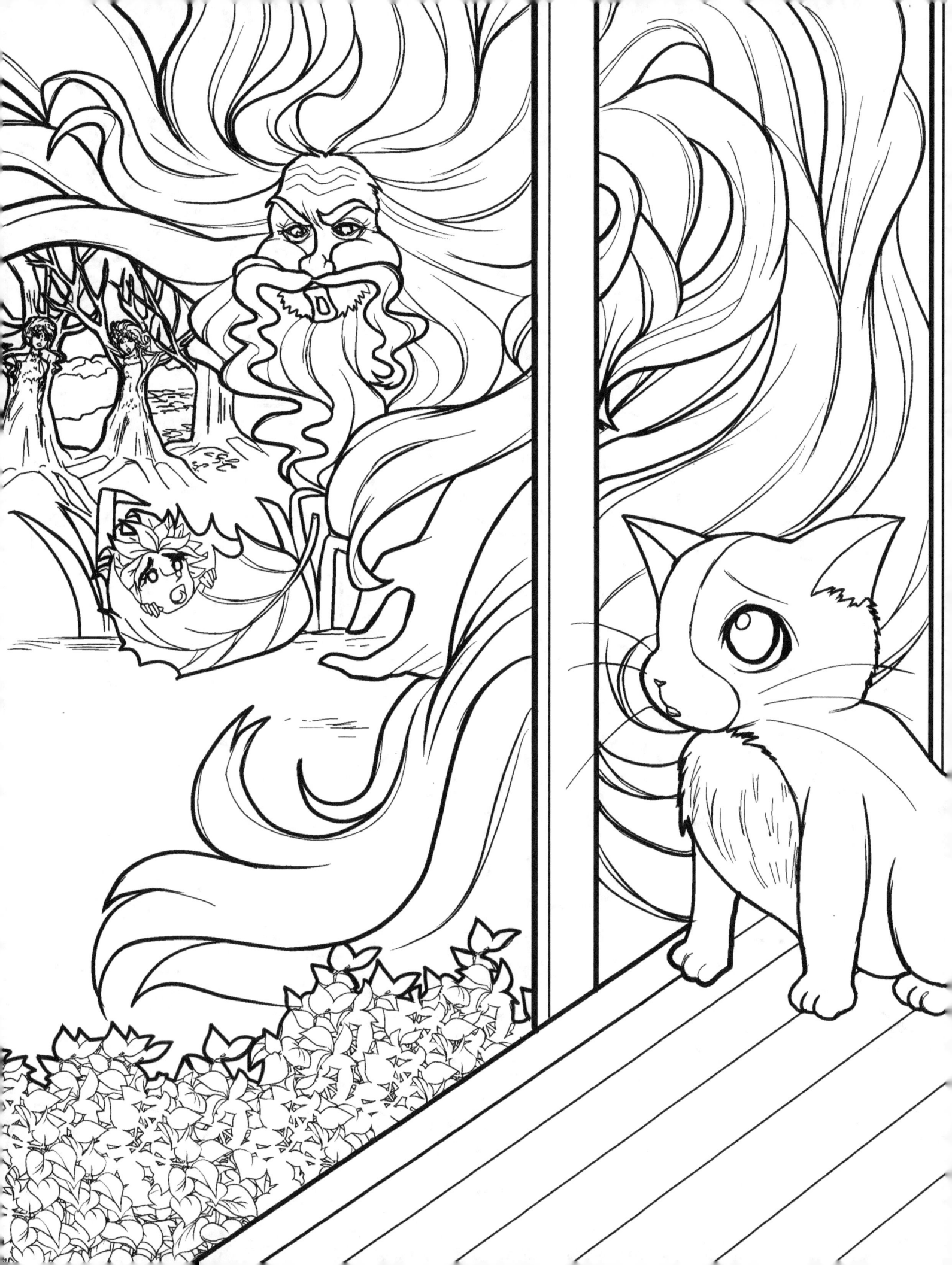

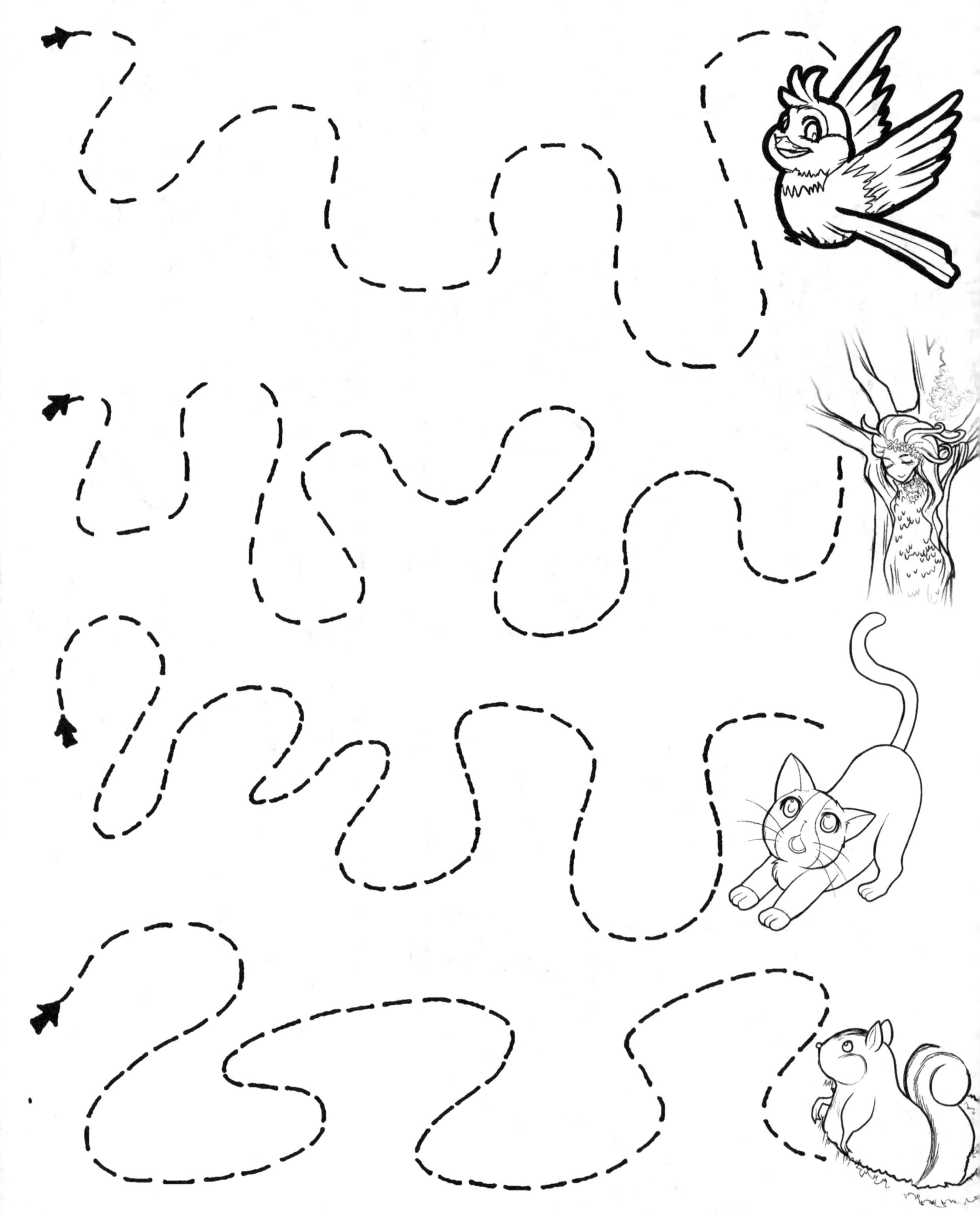

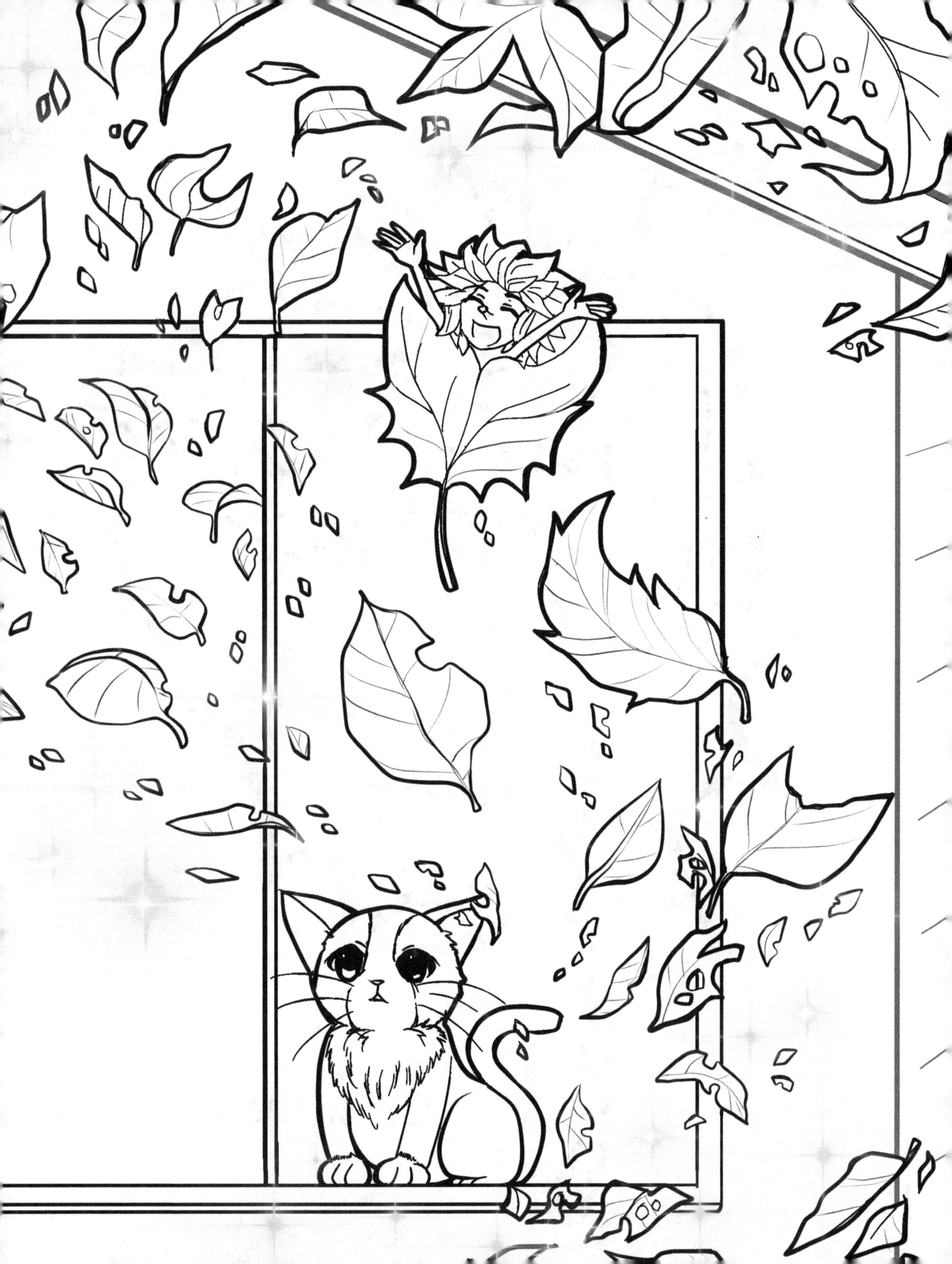

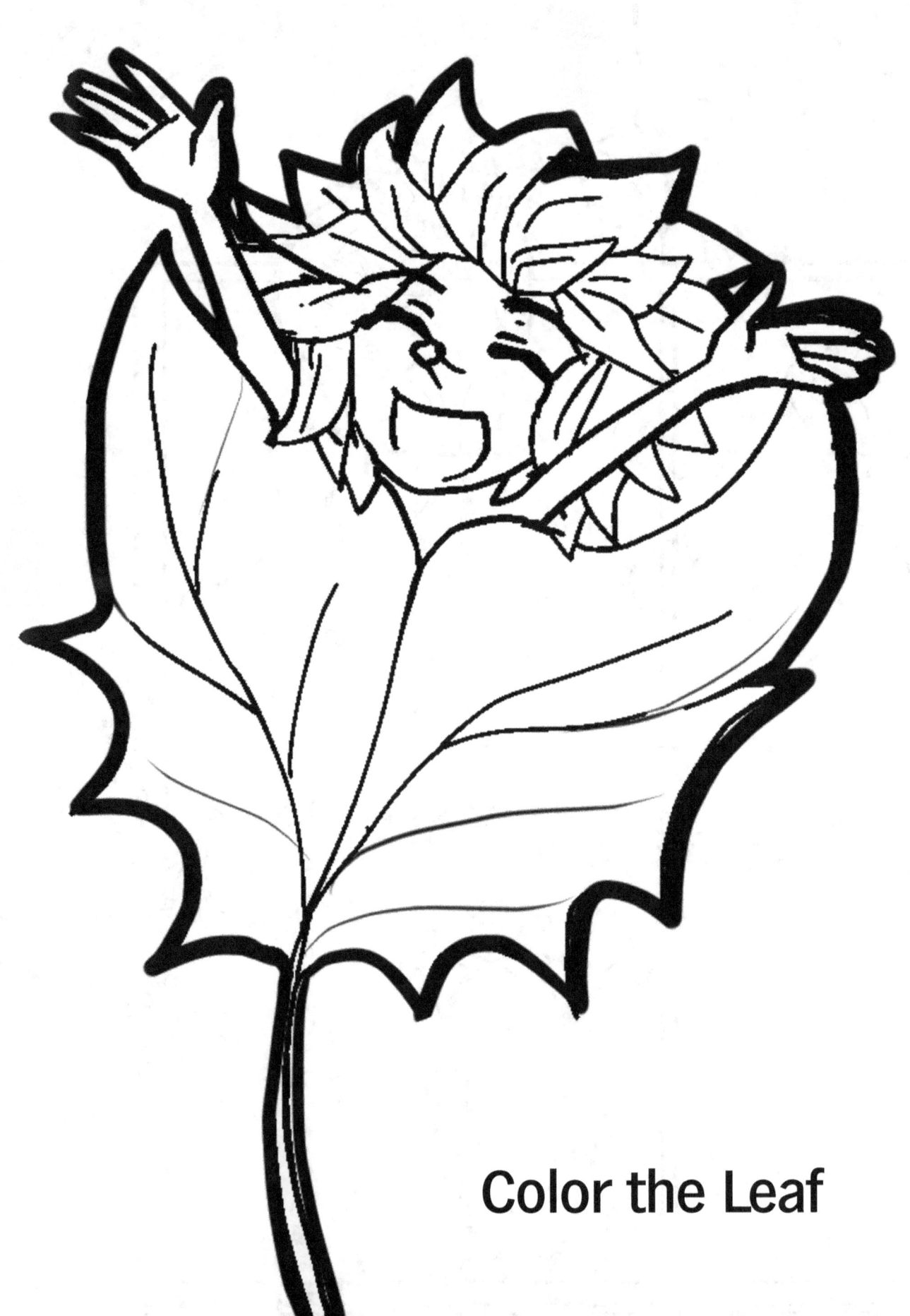

Color the Leaf

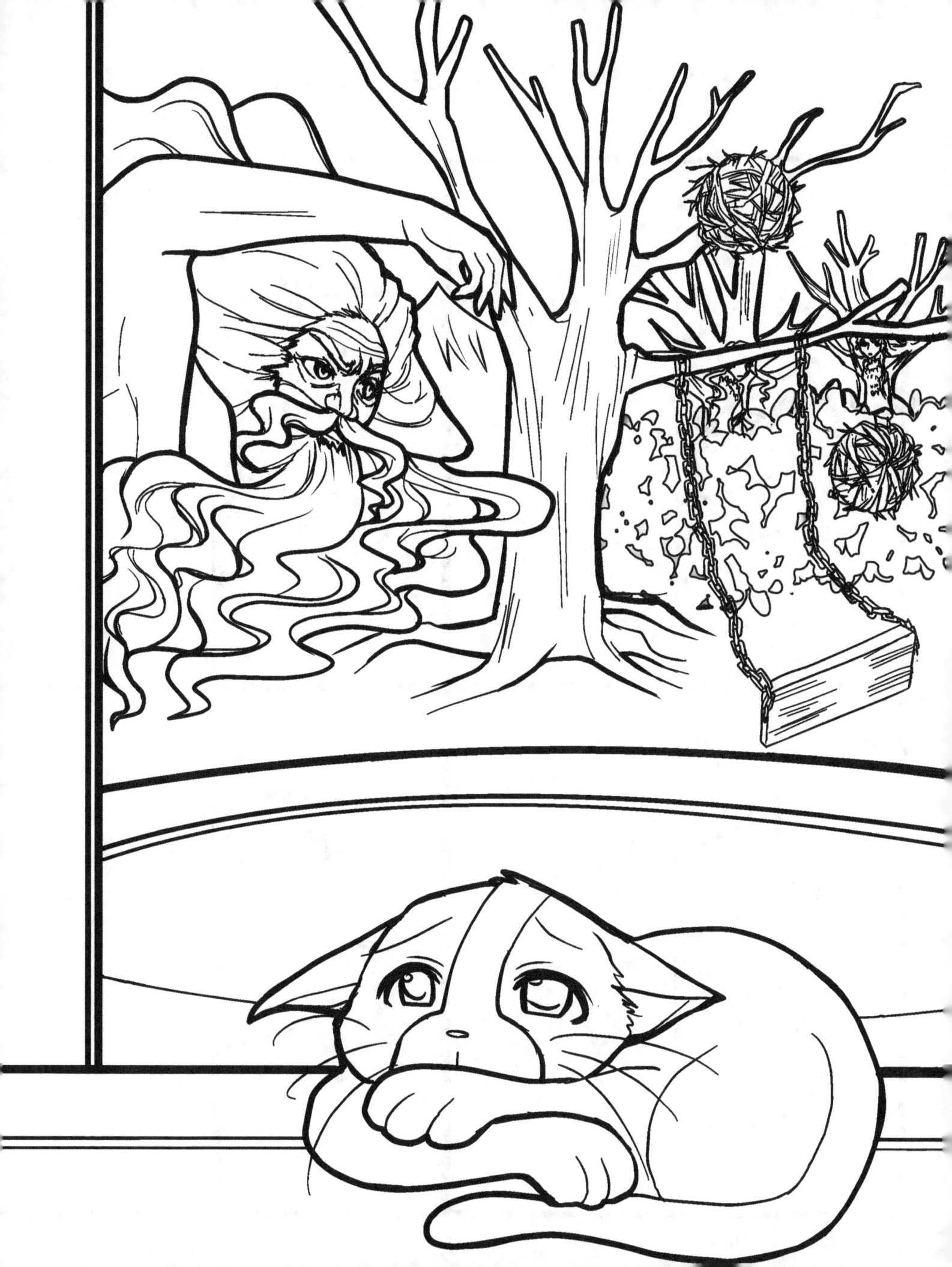

Finish Drawing the Leaves and Color!

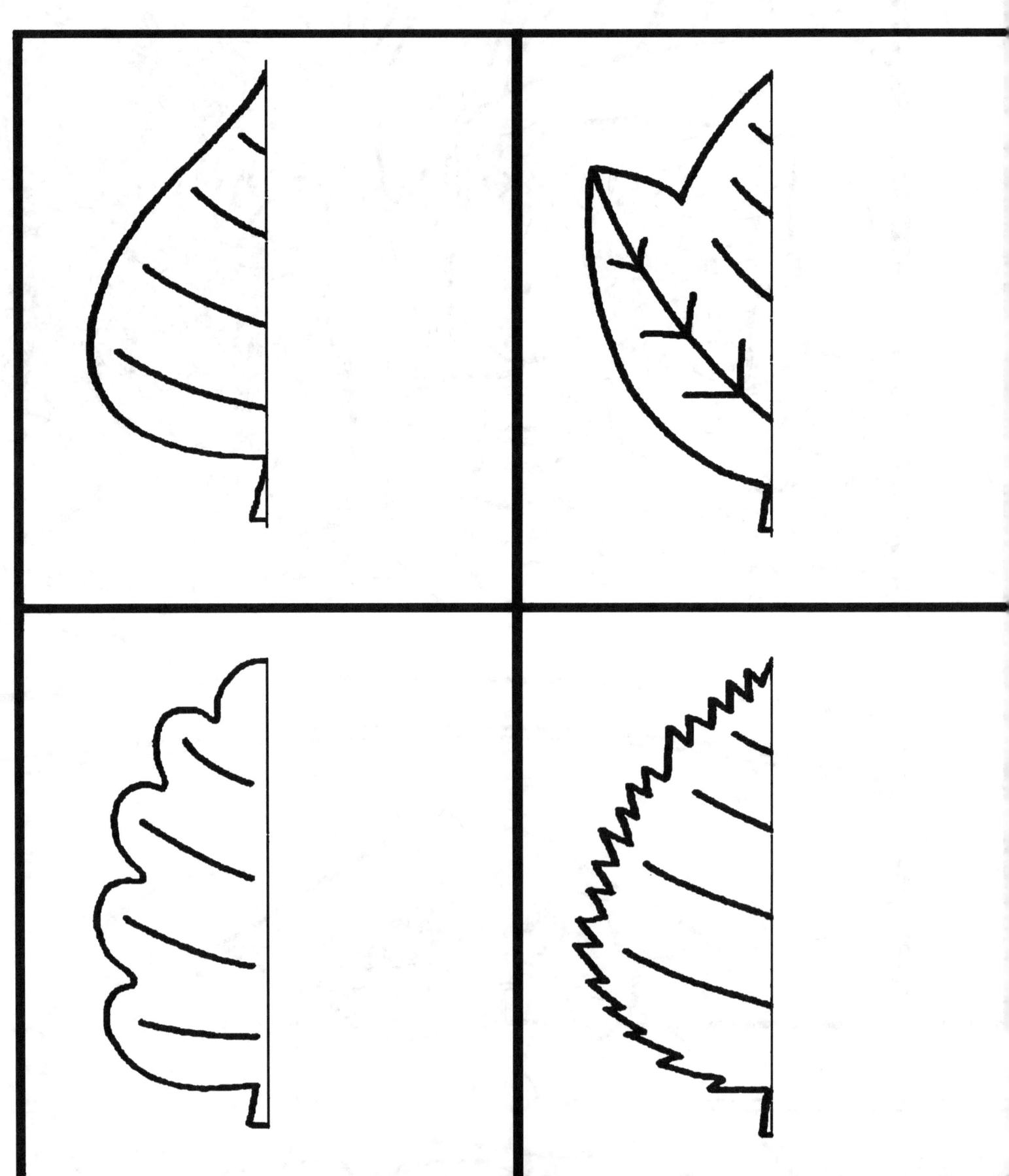

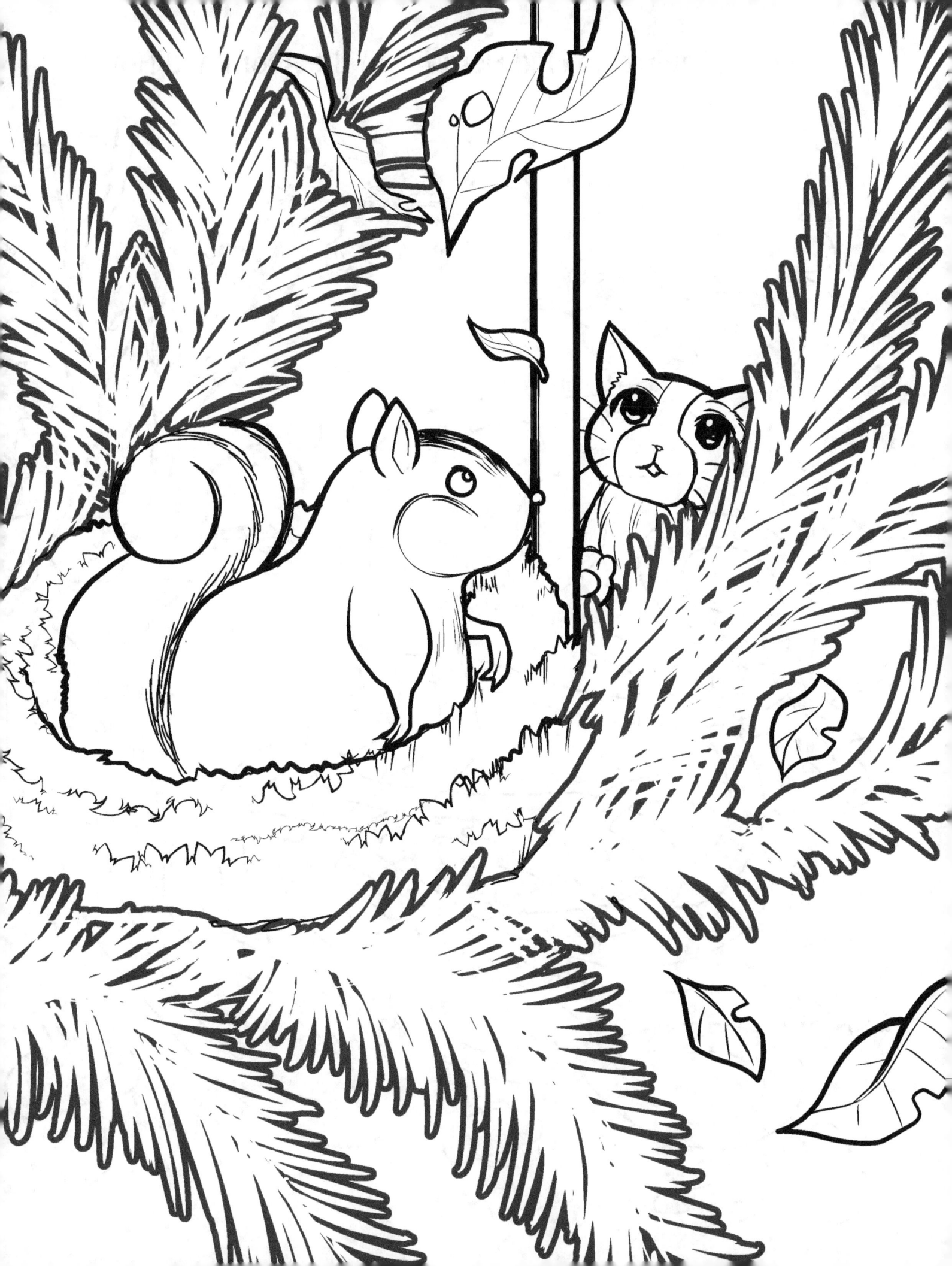

Help the Squirrel to Find Her Way to the Acorn and Home

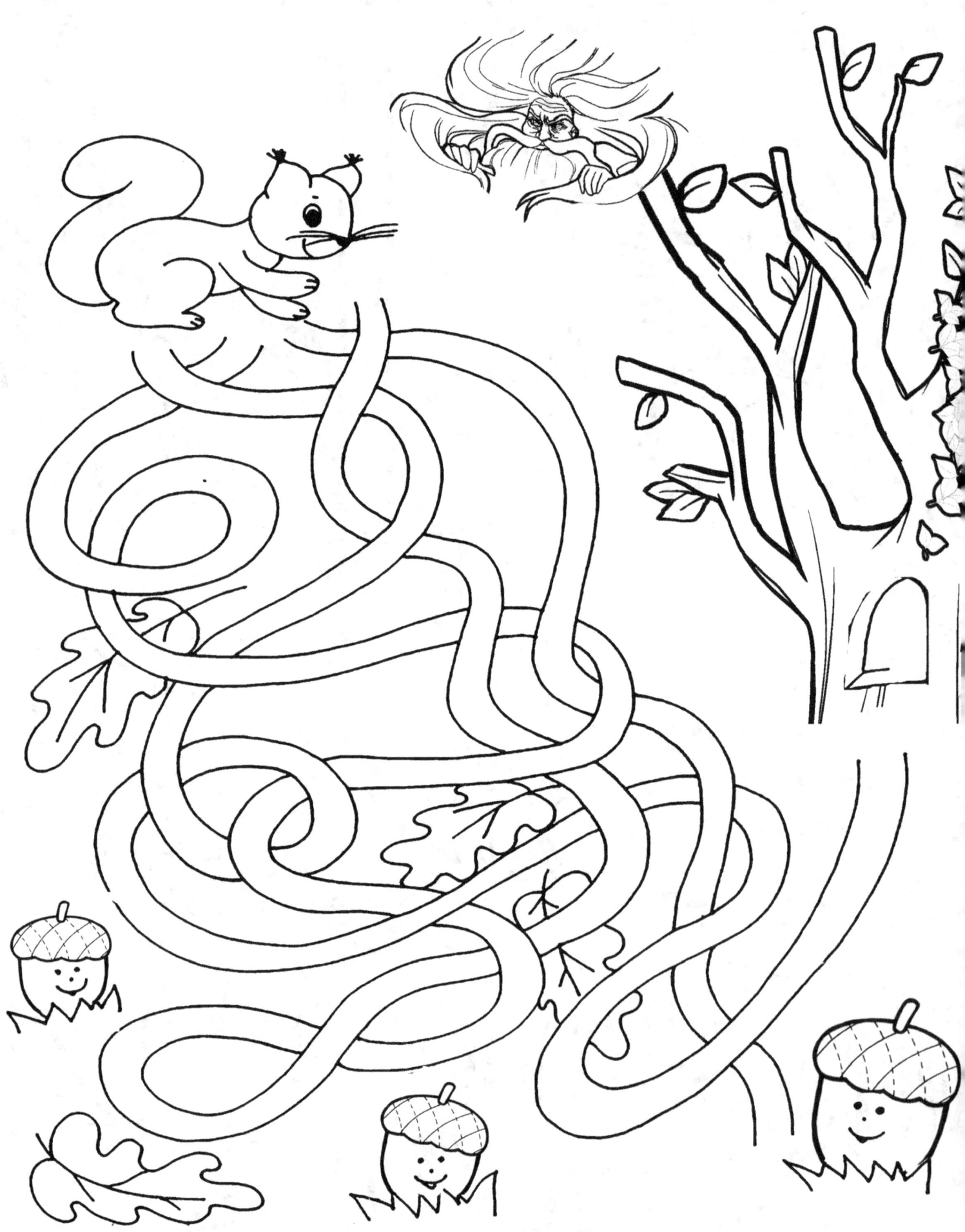

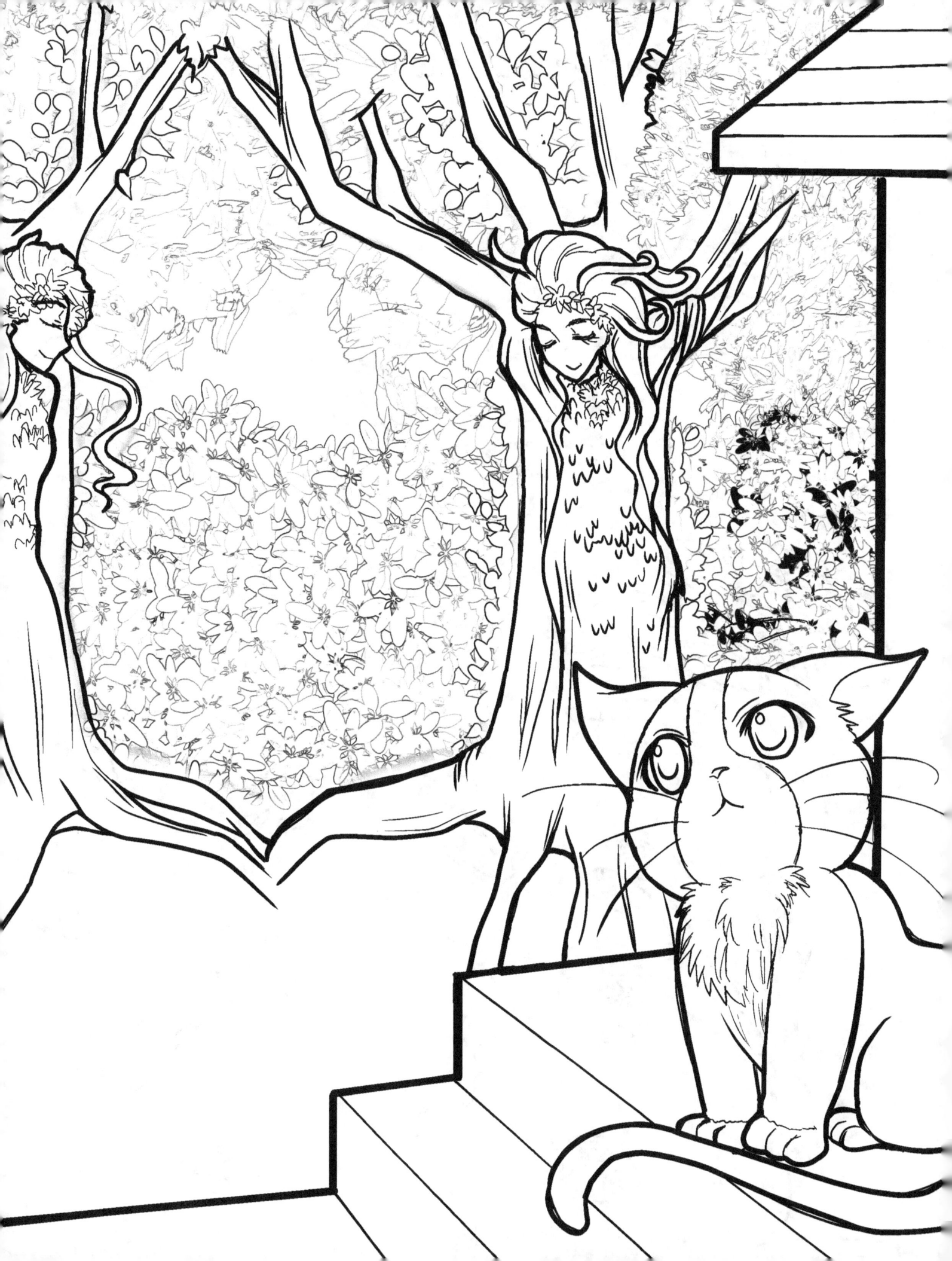

Connect All Leaves to the Right Trees

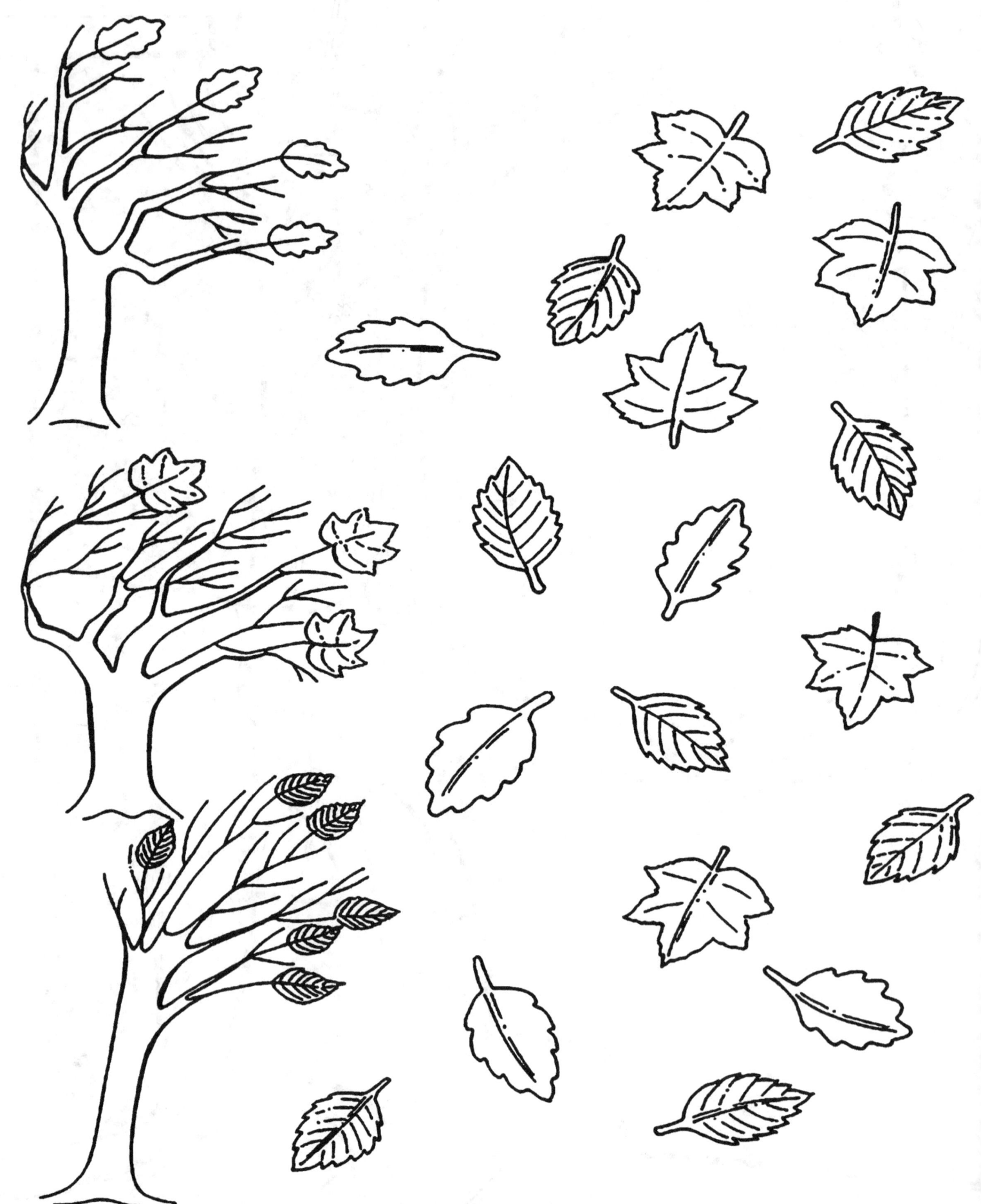

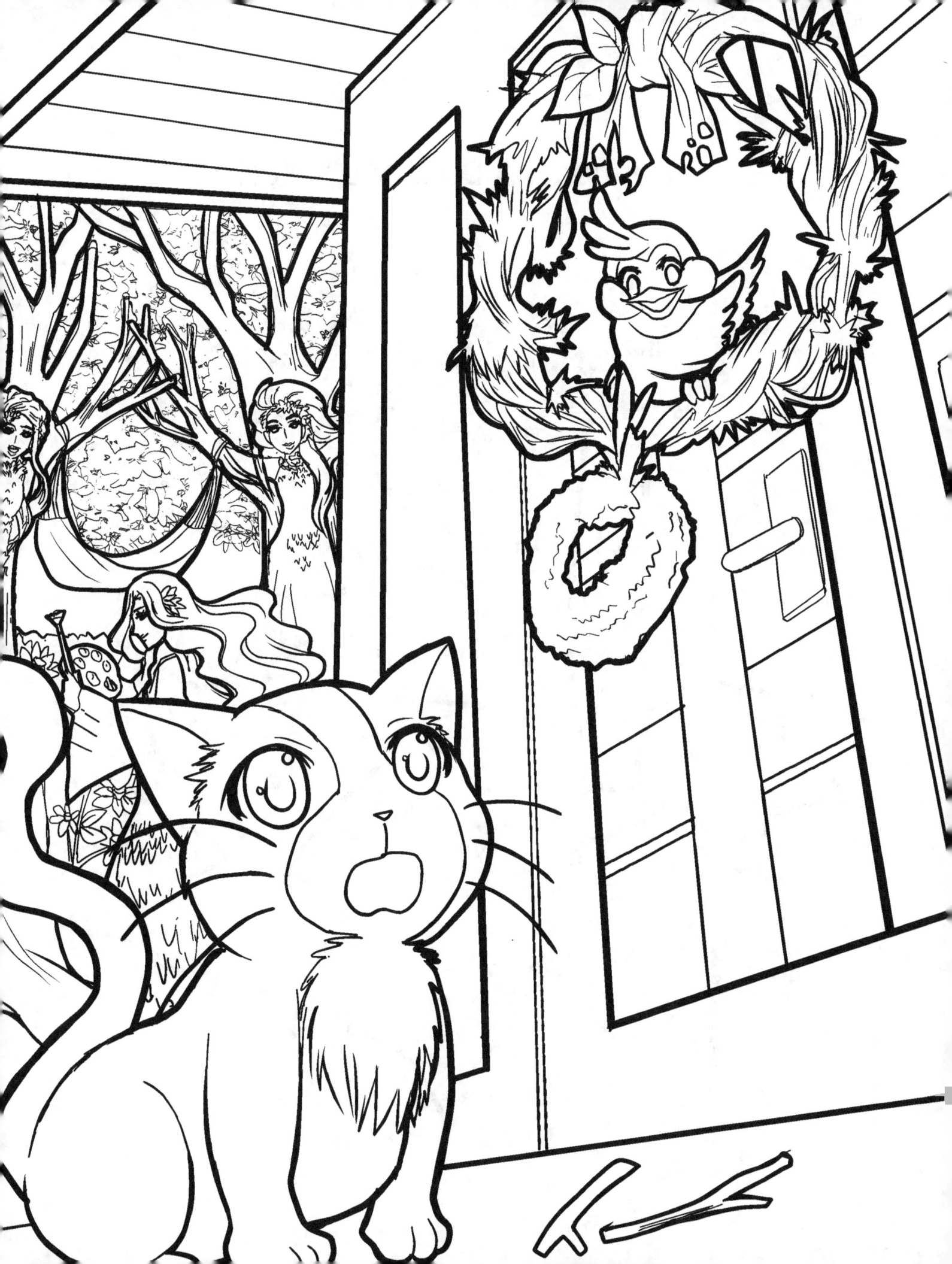

Connect All Dots and Color!

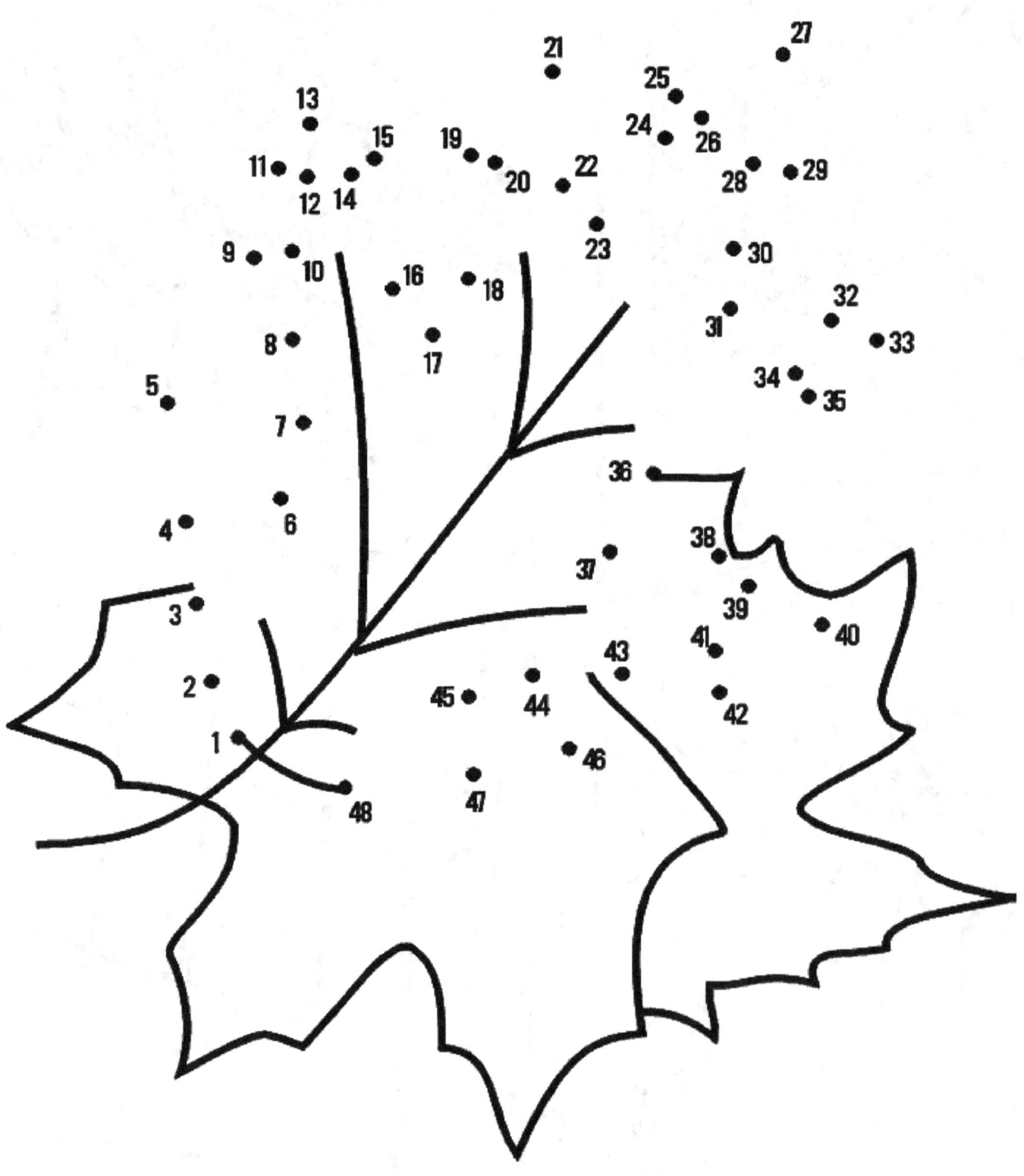

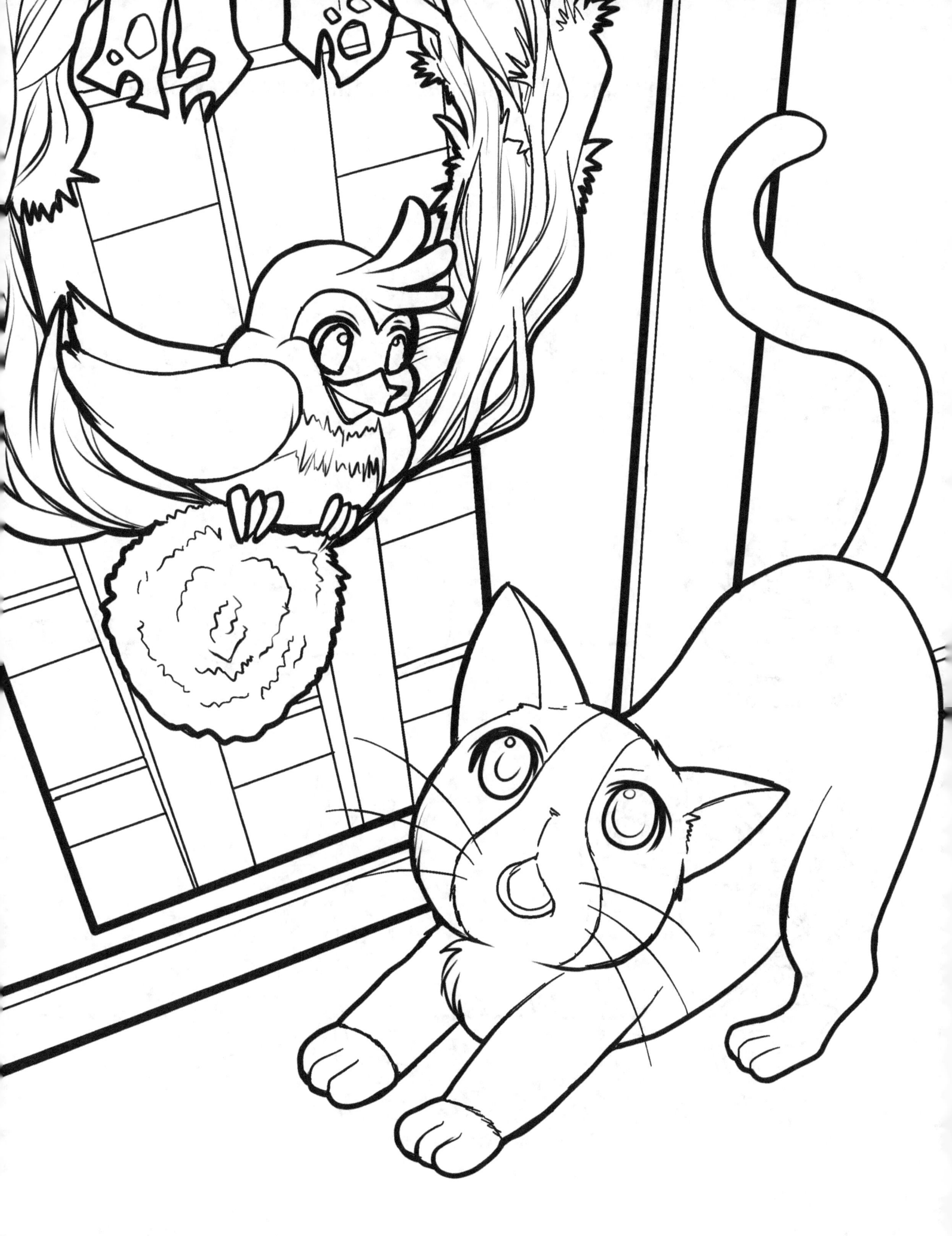

Fill in the missing letters for each of the following words!

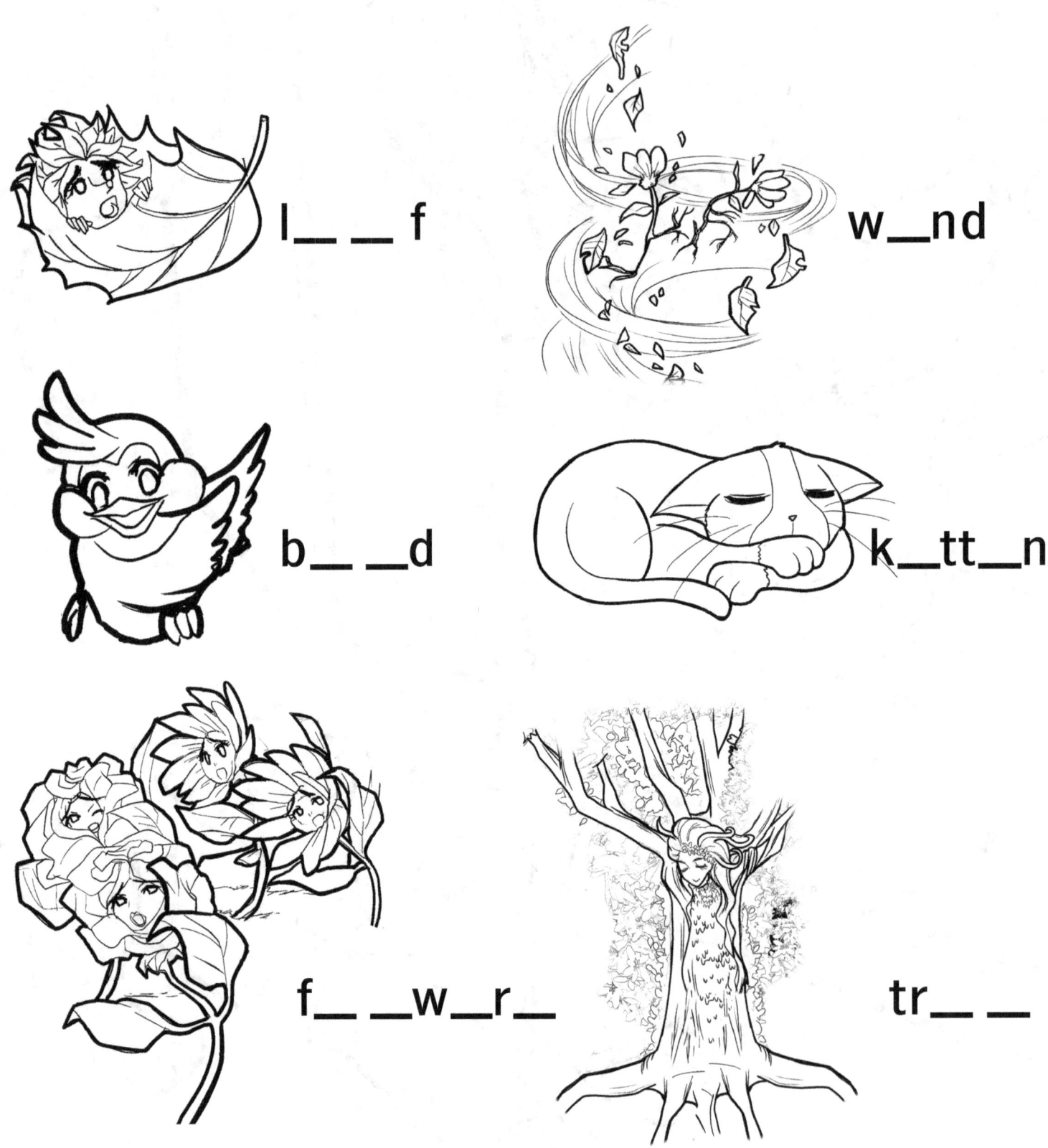

l_ _ f

w_nd

b_ _d

k_tt_n

f_ _w_r_

tr_ _

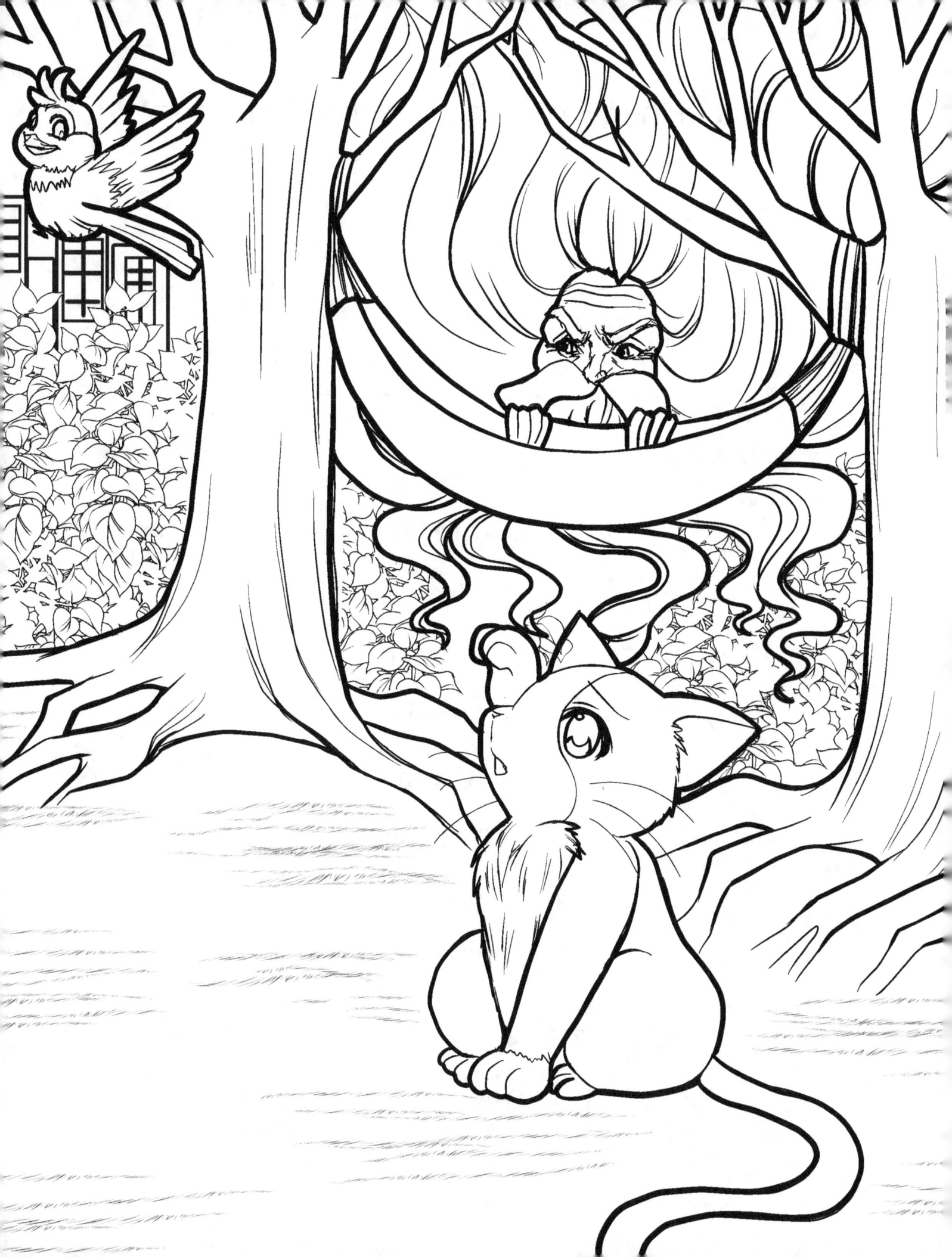

Match the Words to the Correct Characters!

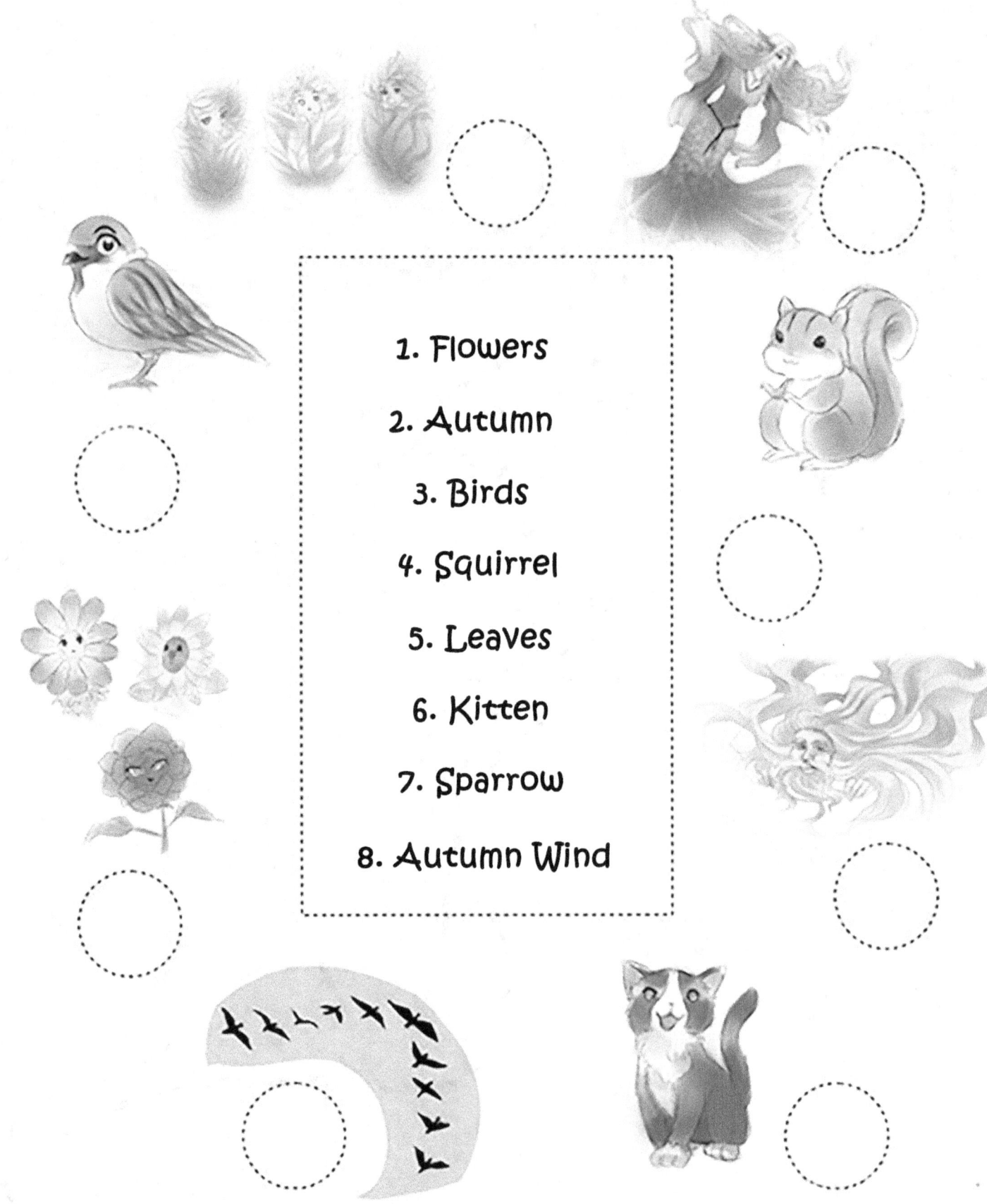

1. Flowers

2. Autumn

3. Birds

4. Squirrel

5. Leaves

6. Kitten

7. Sparrow

8. Autumn Wind

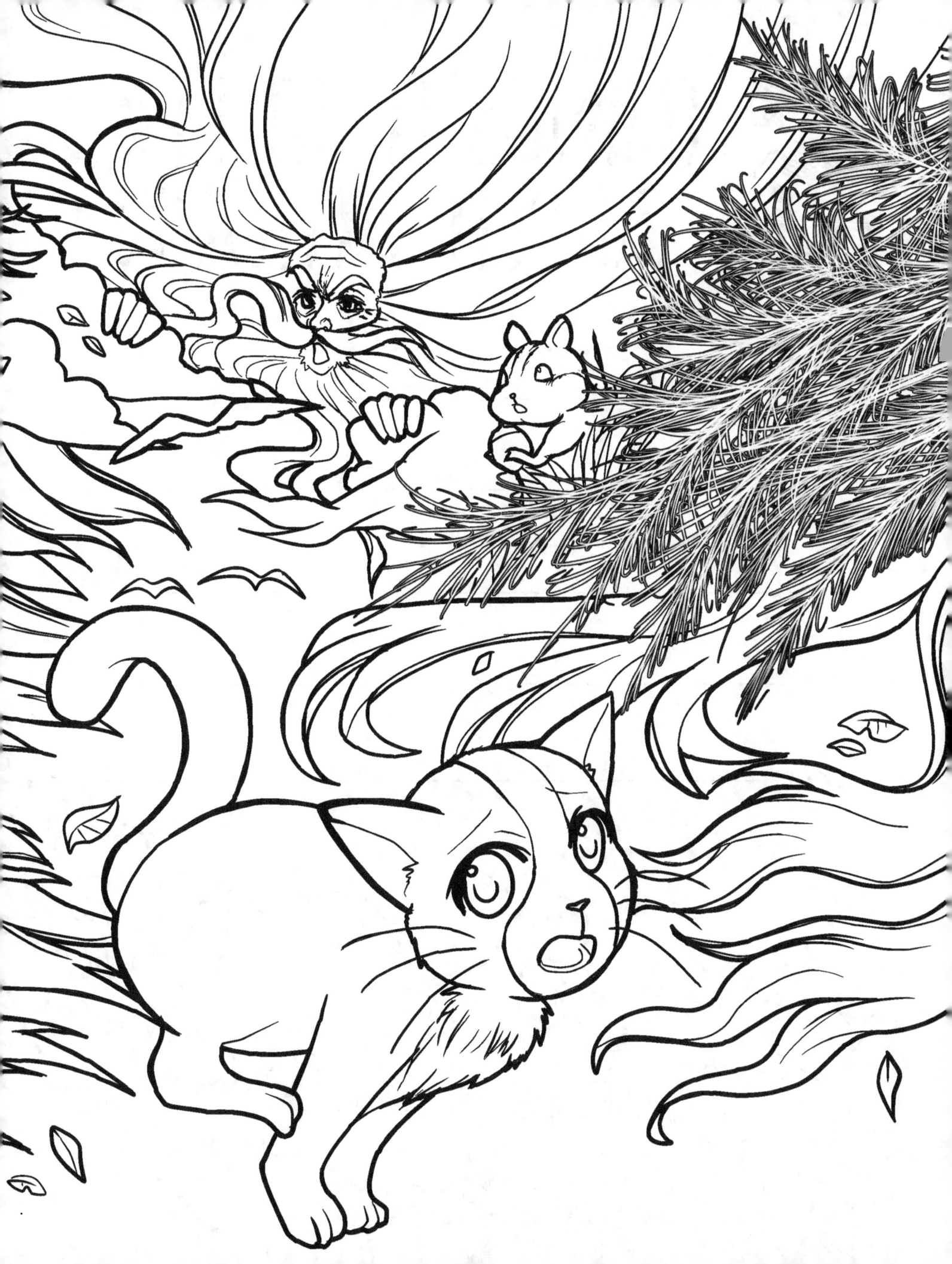

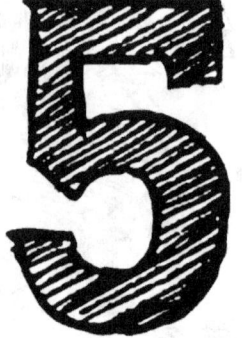 THINGS THAT I LIKE ABOUT AUTUMN...

1) _____

2) _____

3) _____

4) _____

5) _____

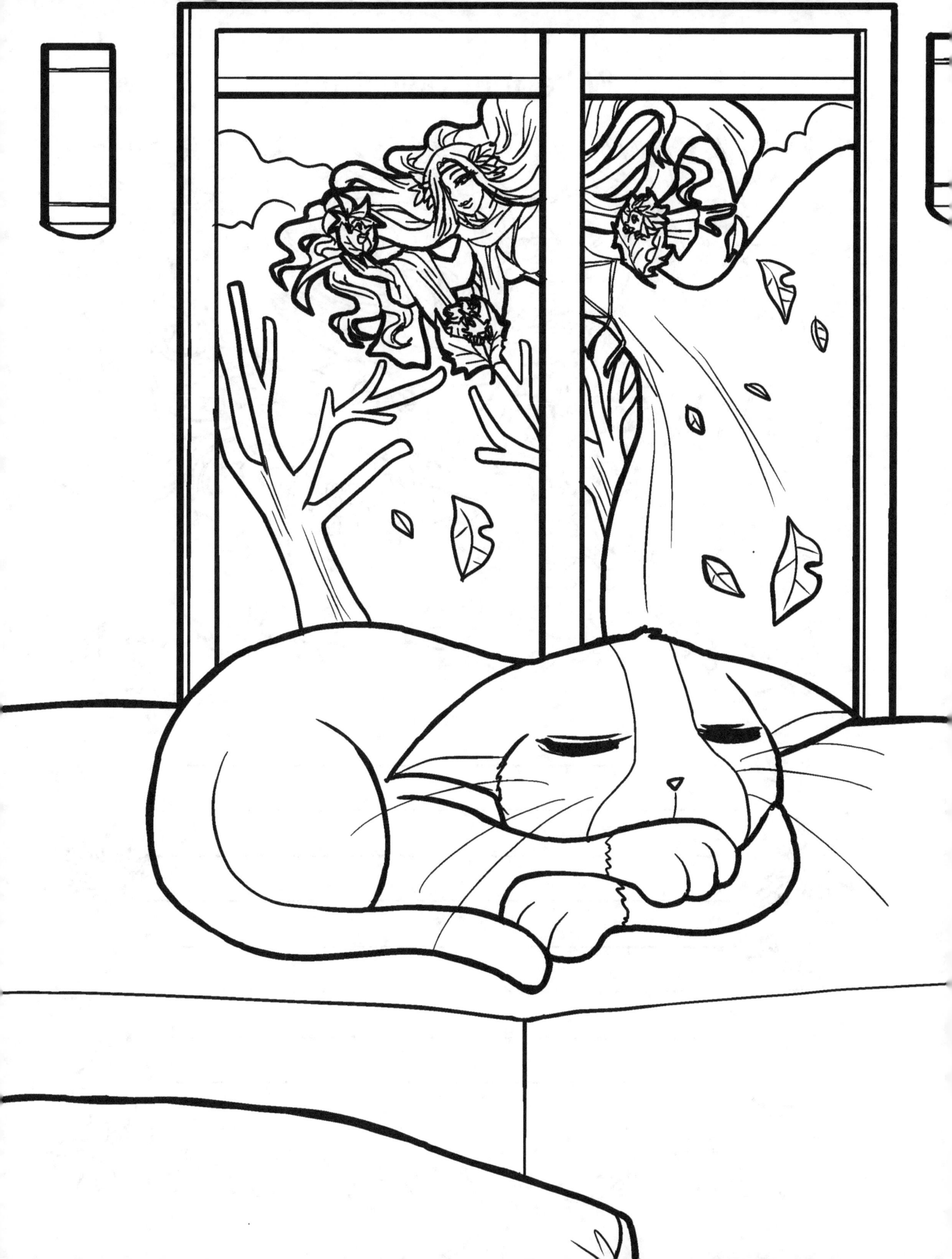

Write Your Own Story

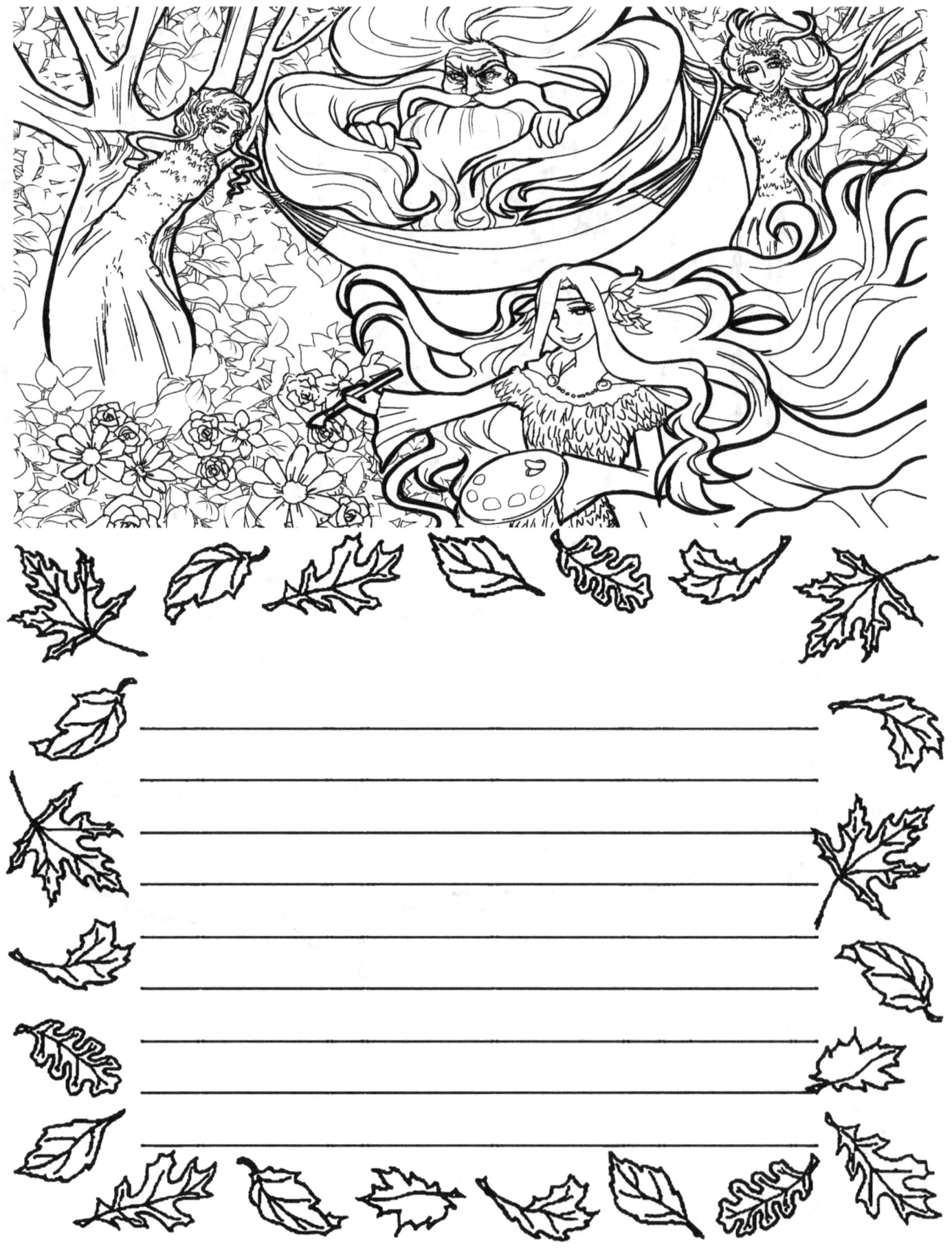

CLOSING WORDS

After you finish reading or coloring this lavishly illustrated children's book, please go outside and explore the sounds, sights, and feelings of the four seasons. It may not be the end of autumn or the beginning of winter, or the first sign of spring or sudden summer heat waves. But if it's the fall transition, when the sky is gray and the leaves are painted in colors of yellow and red, and all it takes is one gust of the powerful wind to change nature from golden to white, don't miss this theatrical stage.

"That Is How Things Are" features repetition and resonance to introduce basic language concepts. Chanoa's expressive artwork illuminates the transformation from colorful autumn to a gloomy pre-winter stage. A rich tribute to both seasons: a fall with blazing colors and the darker symbols of coming winter. Be sure to get young explorers outside into the cold to see the departing autumn with its disappearing leaves.

I hope you had fun coloring this book and enjoyed some activities as you set out on adventures with the powerful wind, the courageous yellow leaf, and the curious young kitten. I would be delighted if (with their parents' permission) young artists and readers would send me their coloring pages and stories so I could see their vision too. You can scan the colored pages and then email them to olga@mrsdbooks.com. I will gladly post them on my blog at Mrs.D.Books. Keep reading and coloring!